CIMA BA3

Fundamentals of Financial Accounting

Study Text

ISBN-13: 978-1973706953

www.astranti.com

CIMA BA3 Study Text

Chapter 1

The Purpose of Financial Reporting

1. What is financial reporting?

Introduction to accounting

Accounting in one form or another has been around for almost as long as civilisation itself. Ever since the early days of trading and commerce, people have needed a system of organisation. Ancient Egyptians and Babylonians both had processes for recording, counting and even auditing their money.

So what is accounting? Broadly speaking, it is **a system of measuring, processing and communicating financial information** about businesses. And it is in this system that ancient civilisations saw numerous benefits. For one, trade and the accumulation of wealth is so much more efficient and more likely to succeed when it is organised. The accounting approach allows you to see through a multitude of transactions to recognise financial patterns and trends that inform you of how money is being used and made.

Types of accounting

Within the scope of accounting, there are two distinct approaches: **financial accounting** (which leads on to financial reporting) and **management accounting:**

Management accounting

This approach focuses on the **processing of internal information so that it may be used to inform management and help them make decisions.** This means that the information must be up-to-date, useful and relevant to the business' directors when making decisions about the business: what products to sell, where to sell the products, which suppliers to use, which assets to purchase, which customer groups to sell to. This ultimately results in such things as budgets, reports on internal costs, product and customer analysis and investment appraisal.

Financial accounting

This approach centres around **the accurate measurement of financial information in order that it be presented to external parties**, such as the bank or shareholders. This means that the financial information presented must be objective, transparent and accurate as they are using it for their decision making e.g. should the bank give the company a loan, or the shareholder invest more funds. This ultimately **results in the financial statements of a company.**

It is the latter of these two approaches with which we will be chiefly concerned.

Fundamental aspects of financial reporting

Financial reporting requires that a number of key activities are undertaken:

Recording data

One key element of financial reporting is recording data. This essentially means **keeping track of transactions and organising them in a useful way**. If you own a shop and you sell books, then you need a system to keep track of sales, purchases, stock, returns and so on.

Whether it is for a single individual or a multi-national organisation, **the basis of financial reporting is the recording of financial data**.

Measurement

Another key aspect is a **standard and repeatable method of measurement**. This means developing a standard approach to almost every aspect of financial accounting.

Imagine, for example, that you wanted to measure the value of a car to record as an asset in the company's books. You purchased it a few years ago for £3,000, but at what price should you record its value in your accounting records now? Where to begin? Most likely you'd try to find how similar cars of the same age and specification are priced and find a current value. Perhaps if you were very clever you'd develop a formula for calculating the average amount of depreciation to apply each year, and use that formula. Or could you even just keep showing it in the books at the purchase price?

There is no right answer of course, but it's vital that every organisation uses a consistent method. Wouldn't it be confusing if we decided to use the purchase price, but the business next door used a formula. We try to avoid problems such as this in financial reporting by using **accounting standards**, which means that **all measurements are done in the same way.** This makes the financial information much more **objective** and **comparable.** That means that when users are reviewing the financial statements the statements are more meaningful to them.

Presentation

Another aspect is a **method of presenting these measurements in a useful and meaningful way,** so that external parties can get a sense of the financial activities of a business or individual without having to go through tomes of invoices, receipts and book entries. The importance here is placed on the **accuracy** and **relevance** of information so that the information isn't misleading or useless.

Summarising

Once you have measured and recorded information, you then need to **summarise the information in an efficient way, so that other people can benefit from looking at the financial information.** This goes hand in hand with meaningful presentation.

For example, let's say you wanted to get a loan from the bank. You turn up at the branch and hand them a thick book with long list of all your transactions throughout the year. Whilst this does contain all the information they need to decide whether you would qualify for the loan, they aren't going to read through a year's worth of your financial activity. So, you need to present it to them in a way that is useful and meaningful to the people who need it, perhaps providing a summary of the sales, profits, assets and liabilities of the business.

Bookkeeping

As we can see, in order for a business to run efficiently it is absolutely essential for them to keep tabs on all of their past, present and future financial activity. As such all the transactions much be recorded and this is where bookkeeping comes in. Bookkeeping is **the practice of recording monetary transactions for a business.**

Bookkeeping is like a financial history of a business, and so good bookkeeping must be **precise, accurate, and thorough.** It includes the practice of double-entry bookkeeping and requires a good understanding of debits and credits something we'll come on to in a later chapter.

Stewardship

The concept of stewardship concerns the responsibility an accountant has to properly look after and present the information and resources of an organisation.

It exists because accountants fill important roles in organisations and have a lot of responsibility. They are responsible for both looking after the finances and accounting information of their organisation, and making sure that information is accurate and useful to external parties. It basically means that **accountants should act professionally and ethically in their job and their performance.**

2. What is a business?

Introduction

Okay, so it may seem a bit pointless explaining what a business is; of course we all know what a business is! However, it is a bit more complicated than you may initially think. Different types of businesses have different rules regarding what they have to report and how to report it, so covering the basics will help avoid any confusion.

As individuals, we aren't generally expected to produce financial reports for our own economic activity. We may have personal accountants or financial managers, but we don't have the same expectations thrust upon us as those put upon a registered business. So what exactly is a business? Well, we can define it quite generally as **an organisation where goods and services are exchanged for one another for money.** Often these transactions aim to achieve some kind of monetary reward (a profit), but that's not always the case.

Different types of business may have different organisational structures, and this is often related to the size of the business. In this section we will look at **the 3 main types of profit-making businesses.**

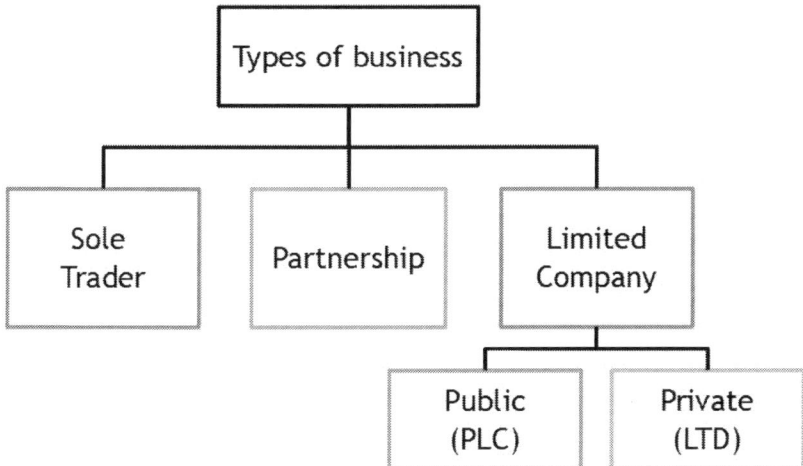

Sole trader

As you probably guessed from the name, this is quite simply **a business that is owned by just one individual**. Another way to think of it is as being self-employed. For this reason they are usually quite small, since they can only afford to spend as much money as the single owner has!

The problem here is that the sole trader is **singularly and ultimately responsible for their finances,** and so they may have to sell assets to cover their incurred debts. They could lose everything they put in and then still have to pay extra to cover debts!

The most common examples of sole traders are **self-employed tradesmen,** or **independent shops and restaurants**. These places are owned and often managed by one person who essentially is solely responsible for their business.

Partnership

Once again, as the name suggests, this one is also quite self-explanatory. **A partnership is a business owned by two or more people**. That's right: not just 2 owners, but any number of owners greater than or equal to 2.

The financial resources of a partnership, as you might expect, will generally increase with the number of owners, since the business has access to a larger pool of money.

So, rather than a person owning a shop or restaurant, you may have a husband and wife, or a father and son, or perhaps a group of friends, who jointly own the business and share responsibility among themselves.

Partnerships face the same problems as sole traders, however, since there is no separation between the owners of the business and the business itself.

Limited company

A limited company is a little bit different. What we have here is an officially registered company that is considered to be legally distinct from the owners. You may have heard about companies being legally recognised as persons. Well, that's what a limited company is; **a company that is viewed as a 'person' through the eyes of the law**.

The concept of separate identity

When it comes to limited companies, it is very important to **separate the company from the owners**. This is why **the business is recognised as a 'person' in its own right.**

This distinction is a key feature of limited companies, and ensures that **the financial activity of the owner is never mixed with the financial activity of the business**. It also means that the owners are 'safe' from losing their personal finances should the business go bankrupt.

Say you were a majority shareholder in an incorporated company, you would be considered legally separate from your company and the company would be legally separate from you and any other shareholders. Therefore, if your company owed a bank £1 million pounds you would not be responsible for paying that money back, only the company would be.

The term 'limited' or 'Ltd' is actually an abbreviation of 'limited liability'. This means that, due to the fact that the business and the owners are legally separate, only the money that the owners invest into the company is at stake. Their personal assets are safe.

This is distinct from a sole trader or partnership, where the entire personal finances of the owners are at stake, since there is no separation between owner and business.

We can further divide limited companies into two sub-groups:

Public limited company

A public company is one that **sells shares to the public, most commonly on a stock exchange**. This means that the company will sell a 'share' of ownership in the company to an investor for money. That investor then becomes a shareholder in the company.

This results in the company having **many owners (shareholders) that have little to do with the day-to-day running of the business**. Ownership here is essentially investment by purchasing a percentage of a company. The shareholder's main concern will be the value of a

share and any dividends paid on the share (a dividend is money paid to shareholders by the company from profits).

Most large companies are publicly listed companies (plc), and the owners will be a number of shareholders who purchased shares in the company on a stock exchange. Apple, Google, Microsoft and Amazon are all public limited companies.

Private limited company

A private company **does not sell shares to the public**. This means that there are relatively few owners, all of whom will be more closely involved with the company. The majority of control usually remains with a small number of owners who play a big role in guiding and directing the company.

Virgin, IKEA, Koch Industries and DELL are some of the worlds largest private limited companies.

Non-profit-making entities

Now, on the other side of the fence, we have not-for-profit organisations (or non-profits). As the name suggests, **non-profits do not set out to make a profit** for their owners.

Like profit seeking companies, **non-profits aim to operate efficiently and to be cost effective**. Not-for-profit organisations include trade unions, charities, clubs, societies and educational establishments. Not-for-profit organisations can exist in both the public and private sector:

Public sector

Public sector not for profit organisations are **owned by the state and are responsible to the government** for their business activities. Public sector organisations can be in the form of a state owned industry or a government run department. For example, The NHS in the UK and The Peace Corps in the US.

Private sector – Non-Governmental organisations (NGOs)

Private sector not for profit organisations have a similar structure to profit seeking companies in that they are owned by investors and responsible to the shareholders/owners. However, **their goals and objectives do not focus on profit maximisation.** Instead, they focus on other goals such as ethical standards and service delivery. For example, Oxfam and The Make-A-Wish Foundation. These organisations are called Non-Governmental Organisations or NGOs.

3. Who does financial reporting?

So, we have an idea of what financial reporting is, and the difference between the main types of business, but how do the two relate? Do all kinds of business use financial reporting or is it something reserved for a particular kind of company?

Well, financial reporting is really a means to an end. As we've seen, financial reporting is all about **measuring, reporting and summarising information, and the result of that is the financial statement.**

A financial statement (or financial report) is the standard way of presenting financial information for companies and we will be looking at these in more depth later on.

Now, anyone can produce a financial statement if they want to, but not everyone has to produce them. In fact, **only registered companies are required by law to produce regular financial statements.** Sole traders and partnerships can produce them if they want, but this is usually as a way for them to manage their finances and help with submitting a tax return.

However, with limited companies, particularly public limited companies, they are **required by law to present their financial information to current and potential investors** in order to show how profitable they are. And, as we will see in the next section, there are a wide range of people who are interested in the financial statements of limited companies.

4. Who uses financial statements?

The people who use financial statements generally fall into one of the groups in the following section. That being said, these groups are not the be all and end all, and there is some overlap between groups.

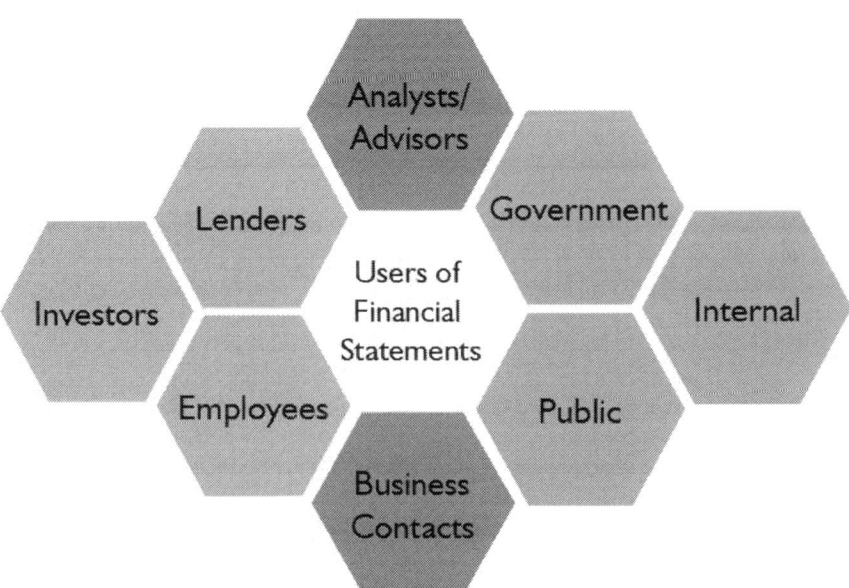

Investors

Who: Existing and potential shareholders.

Why: Investors (or shareholders) use financial statements to look at the overall performance and profitability of the company. As owners of shares of the company, it's only natural that they should be interested in seeing how much of that profit is coming their way!

Investors may also take an interest in the social or economic policies of the company. For instance, if you were to invest in a clothing manufacturer, you may be pleased by the potential profits, but disagree with their policies on exploiting labour in third world countries.

Lenders

Who: This group contains anyone who has lent, or wishes to lend, money to a business.

Why: Lenders will want to know that the business they are lending money to will be able to pay them their money back in the long term.

If a friend asks to borrow £20, but he doesn't currently have a job, and a history of not paying back his friends, then you might think twice about reaching for your wallet!

Employees

Who: Past, present and prospective employees of the company.

Why: Employees are primarily concerned with their employer's ability to pay their wages and pension, but may also be concerned with their future job prospects and security at the company.

Analysts/Advisers

Who: Specialists who generally work on behalf of investors or management.

Why: This will depend on the needs of the clients. However, analysts/advisers usually have more technical knowledge than their client, and so this group essentially acts as the 'middle man' between another group and the business.

Business contacts

Who: Customers and suppliers of a business.

Why: Customers will want to ensure that a product or service can be provided in the future. You wouldn't buy a 12-month gym membership if it looked like gym might go bankrupt!

Suppliers will want to make sure that the product or service they provide can be paid for by the business. So, a cleaning company may think twice before becoming a supplier of their service to the same gym.

Government

Who: Primarily taxation authorities, and also any other government body that needs information for their purposes. For example, taking information about all national business to evaluate the economy.

Why: Companies have a legal obligation to provide financial information so that the government can tax the businesses appropriately.

Public

Who: Tax-payers, consumers and other special interest groups.

Why: This group is generally more interested in the policies of the business. For example, certain public groups and consumers have shown increasing interest in promoting fair trade between large corporations and local/developing suppliers.

Internal

Who: The management and staff, which is divisible into 3 sub-groups:

- **Strategic:** Top level of management (executives, members of the board).

- **Tactical:** Middle management (departmental heads).

- **Operational:** Lower management (supervisors/team leaders) and their staff.

Why:

- **Strategic:** Top level management deal with long-term plans for the business. They will want to know that the business is able to sustain itself for a long time and be profitable as this will impact their reputation as business managers.

- **Tactical:** Middle management deal with short-term plans, such as meeting scheduled targets and deadlines for divisions of the business. They are concerned with implementing the long-term plans of top level management into the day to day activities of the company. The information in financial statements is too high level for them to be able to use it to make decisions, but they may be interested personally to ensure the business is secure and making profits and so their wages and long term job security are assured.

- **Operational:** Lower management deal with day-to-day activity and their staff do the activity of the business. Like the tactical managers, job security and ability to pay wages is key to this group.

5.   Elements of the financial statements

Introduction to the statements

The need to be able to have a reliable insight into the complexities of a businesses finances really came to light during the industrial revolution.

With the introduction of machinery and specialisation (where people became responsible for a single part of production rather than the whole process), this era witnessed significant changes to the way products were produced.

Everything about trade got bigger, the distances travelled, the amount of goods produced and the quantities of money exchanged. Business owners needed to be able to properly monitor their businesses and hold their managers accountable.

Initially, financial reporting was left to be decided by individuals, but in the 20th century there was increased government involvement. **Today, we have in-depth regulations on how businesses should report their finances**.

Financial statements are the window to the inner-workings of a business, and they can give us insight into the **performance** and **financial position** of the world's largest companies, as well as a local butcher or hairdresser.

The statements are compulsory for **certain kinds of business**, and follow **strict guidelines** meaning they are user-friendly, and the financial information of **different companies can be compared easily**.

The financial statements of a limited company will usually come as part of an **'Annual Report'**, and their aim is **to provide a range of information about the performance of the business**, particularly its **financial performance**.

Terminology

Now, before we dive straight into the individual statements, we're going to need to take a look at some of the key terminology that is linked to them.

You will need to understand these concepts in order **understand how the statements work and what they show.**

Assets

An asset is a **resource that is owned or controlled by a company,** that can reasonably be expected to bring the business money.

The most common examples of assets are **buildings, machinery and equipment,** but assets can also be things like **cash, money owed to the business** by customers and **products** that are **in production** or are **ready for sale** to customers.

All of these things can reasonably be expected to bring the business money, since they can either be **sold for money** or they are **used in the business's operations**, which obviously bring in money.

So, let's take J Shoes Ltd – a shoe manufacturer and retailer. This company has the following assets:

- a shop

- a factory (used to produce shoes)

- a warehouse, where it stores its finished shoes, what is known as its inventory

- the shoes that are waiting to be sold in its shop – also called inventory

- the shoes that are half-made and still in the factory (called Work-In-Progress or WIP)

- the material used to make the shoes

- the equipment used to make the shoes

- an amount of cash in the company bank account

Liabilities

A liability is basically money that a company owes or will owe. In other words, a liability is a debt, and therefore the opposite of an asset.

Most liabilities are somebody else's assets! For example, a debt owed to a bank is the bank's asset.

Let's revisit J Shoes Ltd. We know that the company owns a warehouse and a shop. Monthly mortgage repayments are owed on these properties. This mortgage is a liability, because it is an amounts of money which the company owes.

The company also owes money to another business from which it buys leather. This debt is another example of a liability – known as a payable (or creditor).

Equity

To fully explain what is meant by the term 'equity', let's break this explanation down into two stages:

Equity as shareholders' funds

Equity is the **amount owed by the company to its shareholders**.

One way of calculating this is to add up the funds which the business owes the shareholders.

Firstly, we include the **capital (i.e. money) put in by shareholders to buy shares**. At J Shoes, when the company started, shareholders put £100,000 into the business to buy the shares – that's their share capital.

Secondly, the **accumulation of profits over the years of operation**.

Let's imagine that J Shoes made £200,000 last year. That profit is the shareholders' money. £50,000 is paid out to shareholders (in payments known as dividend payments) as a return on their investment. However, the remaining £150,000 is kept in the business to reinvest.

Now, we can see that the shareholders` funds are the initial £100,000, plus the additional £150,000 they've just reinvested. In addition to this, previous profits that have been retained in a similar way total £750,000.

So, the total shareholders' funds for J Shoes is:

£100,000 + £150,000 + £750,000 = £1m.

The business effectively owes the shareholders £1m.

Equity equals net assets

Equity shows shareholders how much money they are currently owed by the business.

As well as adding up the shareholders' capital invested and retained profits we can also work out equity in another way.

Equity = Assets – Liabilities (the net assets)

Let's go back to J Shoes Ltd. J shoes Ltd has assets worth £10m and liabilities worth £9m. So:

£10m - £9m = £1m

Those net assets are owned by the shareholders – and so again represent what is owed by the company to its shareholders. i.e. its equity.

J shoes Ltd has £1m in net assets, and therefore J shoes Ltd's shareholders have equity of £1m.

Income

Income simply refers to the amount of incoming money that a company receives during a particular period.

The most common form of income is the money coming in from sales made. This particular form of income is called revenue.

Other examples of income include the interest received on bank loans and the payments received as a result of investment in other companies.

Let's return to J Shoes Ltd. One month, J Shoes Ltd receives £50,000 from selling shoes. During the same month, they receive interest on money in their bank account totalling £1,000.

J Shoes Ltd's revenue for this month is £50,000 but their income is:

£50,000 + £1,000 = £51,000.

Expenses

Expenses are amounts of money leaving the business during a particular period which are required in order to help the business generate revenue.

Expenses include the various costs of running a business; the cost of actually selling products, the wages, rent on a shop buildings, etc.

All of these costs contribute towards helping the business to make money, and so they are classed as expenses.

Let's look back at J Shoes Ltd. They have expenses on materials purchased, staff salaries, factory rent, machinery repair and so on.

Cash and profit

It is important to differentiate between the ideas of cash and profit.

Let's say you have £1,000 in the bank and you decide to set up a stall at your local market selling hot drinks. To buy all of the supplies it costs you £200 and on the day, you sell enough hot drinks to make £250.

In this scenario, you will have received £250 in cash. This **cash is the amount in metal, paper or digital money that you've received from customers.**

Your **profit, on the other hand, is the difference between what you earn and how much it costs you to earn it**. So here, you received £250 in cash but spent £200 on supplies, so your profit was £50, and you now have £1,050 in your bank account.

Let's take this idea further. Imagine that you paid for your supplies on credit. That means that you will pay for them at a later date. In that case, your cash balance would be £1,000 in your bank plus the £250 you received from customers. The £200 for supplies is yet to go out.

In this case, then, your cash balance will be £1,250. This is because of the time difference between when you received the supplies and when you will have to pay for them, yet your profit is still just £50. After a few months your business has done well but you've yet to pay your suppliers. You now have £100,000 in your bank account but you have actually only made £14,000 in profit in that time.

As you can see there are times in business when the cash balance can be very different from the profit. Of course, eventually, you will pay the money owed and your bank balance will reflect the profit you earned. But, it is worth understanding that your cash balance will not always match your profits and this needs to be considered by businesses in their planning!

6.   The financial statements

The financial statements are essentially a method of **organising and displaying** a company's financial information to make it **useful and understandable** for potential investors.

It is important that the financial statements provide a **true and fair view of the financial position of the company**. This means that the information provided is **reliable** (backed up with some kind of accounting system), is **factually correct and is not biased or distorted**.

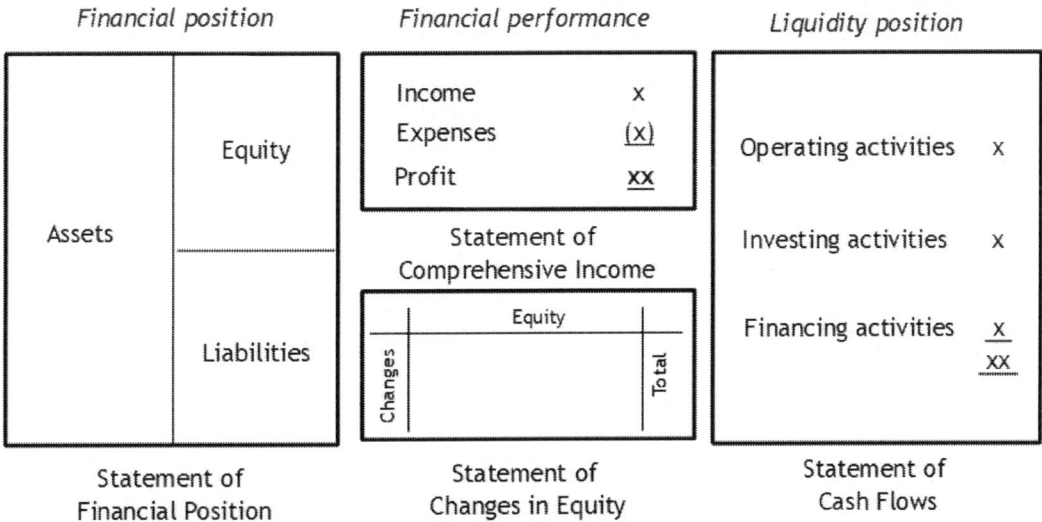

Below are explanations of the most important financial statements.

The Statement of Financial Position (SOFP)

The Statement of Financial Position shows the **assets, liabilities and equity** of a business. It is also known as the **'balance sheet'**, quite simply because it 'balances' a company's assets against its equity and liabilities.

The Statement of Financial Position should **'balance',** and if doesn't, we know that something has gone wrong.

So, J Shoes's accountant is in the process of writing the company's Statement of Financial Position. He finds that the company's assets are worth £10m and the liabilities worth £9m. But, he has calculated an equity amount of £2m.

However we know equity is assets – liabilities:

£10m - £9m = £1m

As we can see, at least one of the accountant's calculations must be incorrect. Something has gone wrong here, and this error needs to be rectified before the Statement of Financial Position can be completed.

The Statement of Comprehensive Income

The Statement of Comprehensive Income, which also goes by the name 'the **Profit and Loss Account', shows the income, expenses and profit of a business over a period of time** (often a year).

It is different to the SOFP in that it **measures and compares income and outgoings** to give an overall **profit for the period**, whereas the SOFP gives a measure of the overall financial position of the business as a whole.

J Shoes Ltd have an income of £1m and expenses of £800,000 for the year 20X3.

So:

£1m - £800,000 = £200,000

So, J Shoes Ltd's Statement of Comprehensive Income would show a profit of £200,000.

The Statement of Changes In Equity

The Statement of Changes in Equity shows the **changes** in the shareholder's **equity** over a period of time (often a year).

The statement shows the amount of equity at the beginning of a period, all the changes to that equity, and then the equity balance at the end of the period.

Let's take J Shoes Ltd. So, at the beginning of 20X4, J Shoes Ltd has an equity balance of £1m.

During the year, J Shoes Ltd receives £1m from investors who purchase shares in the company. The same year, J Shoes Ltd also makes a profit of £300,000, but shareholders also withdraw £100,000 in dividends.

The equity at the end of the year will be:

£1m + £1m + £300,000 - £100,000 = £2.2m

So, at the end of the year, shareholders own £2.2m in equity. That's an increase of £1.2m from the start of the year. All this is what the company's Statement of Changes in Equity will show.

The Statement of Cash Flows

The Statement of Cash Flows gives information on **what a business has been doing with its cash over a period of time** (often a year).

Simply put, the statement shows **where the money that a business used came from,** and what that money was **spent on.**

The statement is generally broken down into three sections which refer to **different areas of the business where cash is used. This separation helps give an even more detailed picture of how the business uses its money.**

The sections are:

Operating activities

This section refers to transactions relating to **a company's main activity.** For most companies, this is **selling products.**

Cash transactions relating to operating activities include the **cash received from sales,** the **cash paid to suppliers** to purchase products or the materials to make the products and the **wages paid to staff** who make and sell the products.

For J Shoes Ltd, operating activities refers to the making and selling of shoes. Cash transactions relating to operating activities include cash received from customers for sale of shoes, wages paid to staff who make and sell the shoes, and the cash paid to the suppliers who sell J Shoes Ltd leather and other materials.

Investing activities

This section refers to the **money spent on assets which will be used by a business in the long-term,** for example equipment or buildings. Because these will be used repeatedly over a long time period to help make the business money, they can be seen as 'investments'.

Therefore, this part of the statement mainly involves the **spending of cash and therefore the total of this section is usually negative.**

For J Shoes Ltd, investing activities might include the **purchase** of shoe-making machinery.

Financing activities

Financing basically means **getting money from sources other than from the sale of its products or services**. This section of the statement shows where a business gets its cash from, aside from its operating activities.

Cash or finance can come from several places, for example **loans** or **shareholder's equity. This section of the statement shows all cash movement relating to financing,** for example the cash received from a loan (when it is received) and the repayment of a loan (when it is re-paid).

So, for J Shoes Ltd, the £1m it's just received from shareholders will go here.

Notes to the accounts

Finally, we have the notes to the accounts. These are exactly what they sound like – **notes to go with the statements, that help to explain the accounting practices used during that period.**

They also provide more detailed information on specific areas of the statements, to help give investors an even clearer picture of how the business works. Though it isn't really a statement in the same way as the previous three, it's still a vital and required part of the annual report.

CIMA BA3 Study Text

Chapter 2

The Accounting System

1. The accounting equation

Some of the more scientific minds among you might be familiar with Albert Einstein's theory of special relativity, often shown in equation form as $E=MC^2$.

This equation is important to scientists because it helps them to understand how energy works. But don't worry, you won't have to know about special relativity for your exams! **As accountants, we have our own important equations, which are essential in helping new accountants to understand how the practice of accountancy works.**

The most basic, yet important, of all these equations is the accounting equation.

The accounting equation

The equation is as follows:

$$\boxed{\text{Assets}} = \boxed{\text{Capital}} + \boxed{\text{Liabilities}}$$

Above is how it is shown in its simplest form, but it is sometimes rearranged to:

$$\boxed{\text{Capital}} = \boxed{\text{Assets}} - \boxed{\text{Liabilities}}$$

This second version helps us to better understand what capital is.

To make sure we fully understand the accounting equation, let's re-examine these terms:

- **Assets – Assets are resources used by a business to gain revenue, such as land, property, materials, inventory, or cash.** These are things that the business owns.

- **Liabilities – Liabilities are amounts of money that a business owes, and can come in the form of loans and various debts with lenders.**

- **Capital** – Capital is the shareholders funds – what the business owes to the shareholders or business owners. It is also known as equity. It is equal to the remaining value once liabilities are subtracted from assets.

Example

Let's take Candy Corner Ltd, which has assets equating to £35,000, and liabilities of £12,000. What is Candy Corner Ltd's capital going to be? Well, Candy Corner Ltd can plug these numbers into the accountancy equation to find out:

Capital = Assets – Liabilities

Capital = £35,000 - £12,000

Capital = £23,000

That was simple!

This means that the business effectively owes its owners £23,000.

Now, the Statement of Financial Position allows a business to use the accountancy equation for all of their assets and liabilities, to find their total capital amount, which is the same as their equity amount.

Therefore, Candy Corner Ltd's Statement of Financial Position will show a total equity amount of £23,000.

In this respect, **the Statement of Financial Position is a representation of the accounting equation.**

2. Ledger accounts

Before the days of computers, financial records were kept in books and written out by hand. This was a time-consuming process which was prone to human error. Luckily, we now have computers and spreadsheets to help us record and process financial information, but, interestingly enough, as accountants we still use the same basic principles and processes that were used before the conversion to digital technology.

Much of the accounting terminology that was used before computers hasn't changed either. For example, we still organise our accounts into 'ledgers'.

The term ledger used to mean a literal book in which people recorded all of their financial transactions. But nowadays when we talk about ledgers we don't necessarily mean a big dusty book of financial information; we just mean all of the recorded accounts of a business!

Let's have a look at what is meant by the term 'accounts'.

Accounts

An account is an 'account of' the transactions made by a business or an individual company, in relation to a specific area of the business. This can be a specific asset or liability, a specific customer, etc.

For example, if Candy Corner Ltd has a 'sales' account, this account will hold all of the transactions concerning Candy Corner's sales in chronological order.

Every transaction shown in a financial statement will refer to a specific account that has been recorded somewhere (i.e. in a particular page in a book, or a particular entry in a computer database).

If we compile a number of different accounts together, we get a ledger.

Ledger Accounts

A ledger is essentially a collection of accounts. And if we put together every account for a business or organisation over a given time period, we have what is called a nominal ledger.

A nominal ledger is a specific kind of ledger that summarises ALL the transactions of a company.

Thus, **the nominal ledger holds all of the data needed for the accounting system of a business to run.**

It is from this data that we can produce the financial statements.

T-accounts

So, we know what ledger accounts are. But how are they presented?

Ledger accounts are divided into two halves: the left side is the 'debit' side and the right side is the 'credit' side. Some transactions are recorded on the 'debit' side, and some are recorded on the 'credit' side.

Because of this, ledger accounts are often called 'T-accounts', since the split between the two sides forms a 'T' shape. Have a look at the example below to see what is meant by this:

T-account example

Debit	Credit

Now if you're thinking, "hold on a minute – what do we mean by 'debit' and 'credit'?", here is the simple explanation:

A debit (DR) is cash received, whilst a credit (CR) is cash outgoing.

This concept is one of the cornerstones of accounting.

To get to grips with how credits and debits function in accounting, let's take a look at the concept of double-entry bookkeeping.

3.   Double entry bookkeeping

For every action, there is an equal and opposite reaction...

Some of you may be aware of Newton's Third Law of Motion, as stated above. It captures the concept that for every event that occurs, there is a subsequent or simultaneous event of equal force to the first. This principle of physics is applicable to double entry bookkeeping, since there are TWO aspects to monetary transactions.

What is meant by this? Think about when you go shopping in a supermarket. **Let's say you spend £50 on groceries. This means that £50 is withdrawn from your bank account for the cost of the groceries.**

This is a loss of money, right? **Yes, you have lost £50 from your bank. However, you have simultaneously gained £50 worth of groceries.**

Have a look at how this transaction would be recorded in a ledger:

Bank		
£		£
	01st Sept Groceries	50

So above we have your bank account (the place where we record all transactions relating to your bank), which has been credited £50 by 'Groceries' (to reflect the loss of money). Credits are shown on the right hand side of the T account.

BEWARE in everyday life we often talk about credit being money going into your bank account BUT in double entry bookkeeping it's the other way around. Confusing I know, but the key is to just learn the rule. Money out is a credit in the bank T-account (and money in is the opposite which is a debit).

Groceries		
£		£
01st Sept Bank 50		

And here we have your Groceries account (the place where we record all transactions relating to your supply of groceries). We can see that your groceries account had been debited with £50 because you have gained £50 worth of groceries.

The £50 you spent has not disappeared, you have exchanged it for items other than money, which are worth £50 (in this case groceries). A loss of money is a gain of something else. Therefore, the transaction has two sides, and both sides need to be recorded.

This is the basic principle behind double entry bookkeeping. **Two entries are made for every transaction, so that both sides of every transaction are shown.**

Debit or Credit?

A term that we haven't mentioned so far, that you need to understand now, is 'drawings'. **The term drawings simply means money withdrawn from the business by its owners.**

For example, if the owners of Candy Corner Ltd withdraw £100 from the company bank account for personal use, this £100 is known as 'drawings'.

So, now we've cleared that up, we can take a look at how we decide whether transactions should be credited or debited to particular T accounts.

Fortunately, there is a very easy way to remember this:

Debit	**C**redit
Increase:	Increase:
Expenses	**L**iabilities
Assets	**I**ncome
Drawings	**C**apital
Decrease:	Decrease:
Liabilities	Assets

If what you are recording shows an increase in expenses, assets or drawings, (or a decrease in liabilities), put it on the debit side of the T-account.

For example, if Candy Corner Ltd purchase £6,000 of candy to sell (which is an asset), £6,000 should be entered into the debit side of the 'inventory' (stock to sell) account, because this side of the transaction represents an increase in assets.

However, if the side of the transaction you are recording shows an increase in liabilities, income or capital, (or a decrease in assets), put it on the credit side of the T-account.

So, when Candy Corner purchase £6,000 of candy to sell, they use the company bank account for their purchase. Therefore, £6,000 should be entered into the credit side of their

company bank account because money is an asset, and spending money is a decrease in their assets, which as we can see should be shown as a credit.

As you can see, these are the two sides of the same transaction.

You will often hear the above memory trick referred to as DEAD CLIC – notice how this works with the bolded letters on the diagram above.

DEAD CLIC is a useful acronym to help accountants remember how double-entry bookkeeping works.

Let's test a few examples to show you how it works…

Scenario 1 – Taking out a loan

So let's start with something easy. When Candy Corner Ltd take out a loan from the bank, they are creating a liability (the money you owe to the bank) but also receiving the cash, which is an asset. For the sake of simplicity, we'll ignore interest in this example.

Let's see how this works:

		Bank		
		£		£
Date	Loan	XX		

The money has gone into Candy Corner's bank, and so needs to be recorded in the bank account. **They have an increase in assets (the cash) which we know is a debit.**

		Loan		
		£		£
			Date	Bank	XX

Here we have recorded the corresponding half of the transaction in the debt account (where we record all transactions relating to debt).

As previously have mentioned, **the debt itself is a liability, and DEAD CLIC tells us that an increase in liabilities needs to be recorded on the credit side.**

Scenario 2 – Inventory purchases

So what's happening when Candy Corner Ltd buy products to sell? They are spending money but acquiring goods which you will be able to sell.

Let's imagine Candy Corner Ltd purchase some candy using cash, to see how this transaction will be recorded:

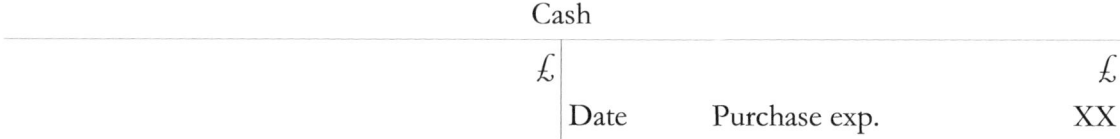

Cash

	£			£
		Date	Purchase exp.	XX

All transactions relating to cash will be recorded in the cash account. Cash is an asset. This means when Candy Corner Ltd spend cash, they are decreasing an asset. Since DEAD CLIC is based on increases, accountants immediately have to be careful, but let's think... **a decrease in assets is the opposite of an increase in assets, and so it is actually on the credit side.**

Candy Corner Ltd must therefore credit the purchase in the cash account.

Purchase expenses

		£		£
Date	Cash	XX		

The products we have bought to sell are known as 'inventory'. The purchase of stock is one of the costs associated with running a business and so is an expense. This transaction should therefore be recorded in the purchase expenses account.

We will look at the concept of inventory in much more detail later on, but for now just remember that **inventory is what we call all the things a business is holding for sale as part of its ordinary operations.** Candy Corner Ltd has lots of candy to sell – this is the company's inventory.

With this transaction, we have increased our expenses to purchase our inventory. Therefore, the corresponding entry to the cash entry must be a debit to the purchase expense account.

By now it should be clear that **one side of a transaction is always a credit, and the other side is always be a debit.**

4.   Documentation and transactions

Source documents

For every transaction a business makes, there must be documented evidence.

You have probably received some of these yourself as a customer, in the form of a receipts from shops. If you haven't, don't worry, the concept of receipts will be explained.

There are actually several standard kinds of documentation and evidence that accompany different stages of business transactions.

They are as follows:

1. Quotations

These are **documents issued by the seller that detail the price of the goods that a customer requires from the transaction.**

These documents are used to establish the price of a purchase. A customer can compare quotations from several different suppliers (sellers) to find the cheapest price.

For example, say Mr X runs a business building wooden furniture sets and selling them online. Before he buys wood for his furniture sets, he is going to see what price the kind of wood he wants is being sold for.

Therefore, Mr X will get a number of quotes from different wood suppliers to compare.

2. Purchase order

A purchase order is **a document which details a request to purchase certain items sent to a seller by a prospective buyer.**

The purchase order will contain information about the supplier, as well as the agreed-upon price, the desired goods and the quantity of goods, and any terms and conditions attached to the order.

Let's say, as the producer of wooden furniture sets, Mr X wants to buy 10 standard sized sheets of walnut wood from a wood supplier, and that comes to £1,000. This is Mr X's purchase order and he will send this to his chosen supplier.

3. Sales order

A sales order is essentially **a documentation of the sale from the perspective of the seller.** It is a confirmation that the order has been received, accepted and is being fulfilled, for the seller's records.

It is a document containing all of the same information about the order as the purchase order – items ordered, quantity, price, terms and conditions.

In Mr X's case his supplier may produce sales orders internally to record the sale, and may send him a sales order as confirmation that the sale is being processed.

A copy of the sales order is sometimes sent to customers along with the goods, and therefore can be referred to as a substitute invoice (proforma invoice), by the purchaser, before the official invoice is received.

We will come to what an invoice is in just a second.

4. Goods dispatched note

This is documentation that is **sent out to the customer to confirm that the ordered items have been sent.**

The goods dispatched note may be sent electronically, for example via email. In fact, many of you have probably received these via email when buying from online retailers such as Amazon.

However, if the goods dispatched note is sent by post, it is usually sent separately to the items; being paper it often arrives before the items and lets the buyer know that they are on their way.

Because the note arrives before the items themselves, it is a good way for the buyer to double-check that the order is correct. It is also a way of letting a buyer know in advance if any of the items requested could not be supplied by the seller.

So, going back to Mr X the furniture producer, in the goods dispatched note from his wood supplier, Mr X will be told that 10 sheets of walnut wood have been dispatched and that this order costs £1,000 (plus any delivery or administration costs).

5. Goods received note

Once the goods arrive, the buyer will send a goods received note to the seller as a way of confirming the receipt of the goods.

This will essentially be a note from Mr X to his supplier, to tell them that the wood has arrived as expected (if it has).

6. Invoice

Once a supplier has received confirmation that the goods were received in satisfactory condition, they will issue a request for payment to the recipient of the goods. This is known as **the invoice**, and is basically a way of saying, 'You've received your item, now pay up!'

So, say Mr X has got his wood as expected and has sent off his goods received note. He's then issued with an invoice detailing the amount he owes for the goods, which is £1,000.

In some cases, like with regular orders, a copy of the invoice may also arrive with the goods.

7. Remittance advice

Once a buyer receives an invoice, they'll then have to pay up (if he was lucky enough not to have to pay in advance)! **Remittance advice is a letter sent by a customer to a supplier, to inform the supplier that their invoice has been paid.** If the customer is paying by cheque, the remittance advice often accompanies the cheque.

So, once Mr X has paid what he owes to his wood supplier, he will send them remittance advice!

If a business regularly orders from the same supplier, they may receive a statement from their suppliers at the end of a certain period, and pay all of their invoices at once, once the statement has been received.

In any case, once invoices are paid, a remittance advice needs to be sent.

8. Credit note

Credit notes are issued by a supplier to a customer in the event that the order cannot be fulfilled or that the customer received faulty or incorrect goods.

Let's say that 2 of the 10 sheets of wood Mr X received were damaged, he would report this to the supplier and they would issue Mr X with a credit note for the damages, meaning the amount he paid (or is yet to pay) for the items on the original invoice will be refunded to him once the invoice is paid.

Again, with regular orders, a copy of a credit note may arrive along with a copy of the invoice or with the order itself, if the supplier is aware that they were unable to provide all of the items ordered and the payment has already been made.

9. Debit note

This is the counterpart to the credit note, in which the buyer confirms receipt of the credit note.

So, once the wood seller has sent Mr X a credit note for the damaged sheets of wood, he may confirm he has received it by sending a debit note.

10. Statement

The purchaser will then receive a statement with a breakdown of what is owed.

These are often issued at the end of the month and if the buyer has made multiple orders from the same supplier during that month, all of these orders will be listed on there.

So, for instance, if Mr X returns 2 of the sheets, the new amount owed will be £800 and this will be reflected in the statement.

11. Receipt

The last piece of documentation in this chain is the receipt. **This is issued by the selling company as a confirmation of payment received.**

Below is a diagram which shows all of these documents, and their place in the chain of documentation which accompanies a transaction:

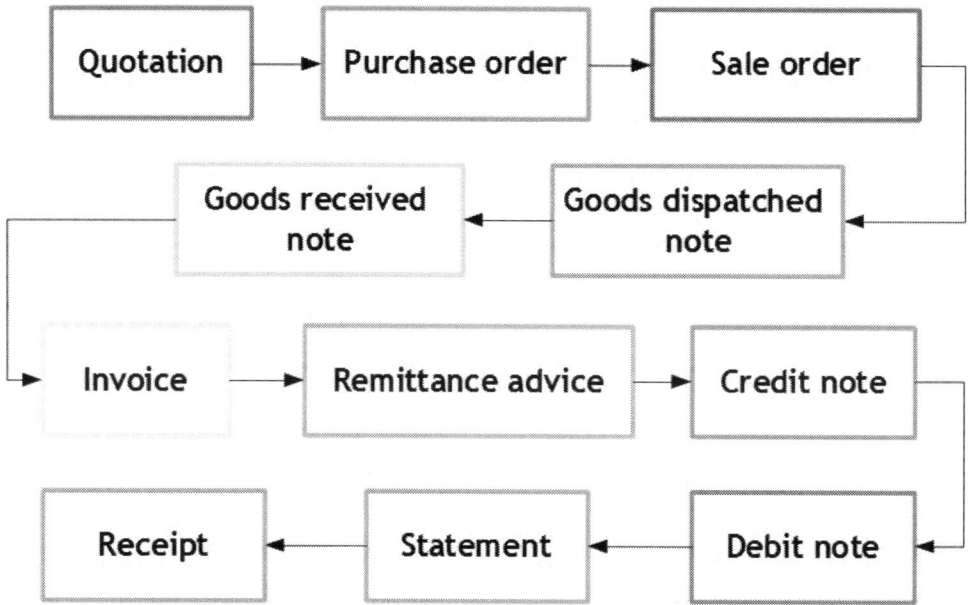

Note: some businesses may not use all these different types of documentation, it all depends on the business and what their needs are.

5. Benefits of accounting systems

It seems like a lot of work and effort to maintain an accounting system for a business. Is it really worth it?

Yes, it is! There are a huge number of reasons why keeping an accounting system benefits a company. Here are the most prominent of those:

Ease of access

An accounting system means that information about business transactions can be accessed easily and quickly. This is not only efficient, but will also aid in speedy decision making.

The systematic recording and presentation of financial data means that we have much quicker access to important financial information.

Relevant information for decision making

Details of business transactions can be stored in the accounts, giving the business a wealth of relevant information for decision making.

For instance, if a company finds that its bank balance is a bit lower than expected based on budgeted calculations, the business has a history of transactions available to check to find the reason why. Such a task would be difficult without the relevant information.

Helps in preparation for statements

When the ledger is balanced and accounts are closed off, a business will end up with a nice simple list of account balances.

When an account is closed off, it means the accountant has found the total amount that can be attributed to that account at the end of a period, be that a debit amount or a credit amount. This is the balance.

A balanced ledger means that all the credits and all the debits add up to the same amount – meaning there has been no incorrect entries into the ledger.

Don't worry too much about the concept of closing accounts and balancing the ledger at the moment, we will look at these later in more depth. **Just remember that having a balanced ledger and totals for each account essentially gives a business a quick list of assets and liabilities for the business, which can easily be turned into the financial statements.**

Furthermore, when all of the ledger accounts are balanced, a business will have a list of outstanding balances for each account, allowing them a quick insight to where their assets and liabilities lie.

This summary can then be easily used in the preparation of the financial statements.

For example, in the summary of Candy Corner Ltd's assets (which was made by totalling up the balances of all of the business's asset accounts) the company can see that its total assets have increased from £35,000 to £37,000 during the year and that they have made a profit of £35,000, up from £20,000 last year.

Now they have the total of £37,000 already figured out and recorded, ready to put into their financial statements and they can also see that profits are increasing which is good news for them.

CIMA BA3 Study Text

Chapter 3

The Bookkeeping Process

1. The bookkeeping process

Introduction to bookkeeping

Nowadays, bookkeeping is largely an automatic process. As soon as transactions are made by a business, they get automatically entered into a computerised system that sorts them into the correct places and handles the double-entry in a sophisticated manner.

However, it hasn't always been like this; as we know, the practice of accountancy pre-dates computers by a long way. Before the days of computers, accountants had to record transactions in books by hand – which probably sounds like a very long and laborious task to you!

Because financial information was once simply recorded by hand, accounting used to be a lot more prone to human error. Therefore, before computerised systems, accountants avoided entering transactions directly into a business's nominal ledger as soon as they occurred.

The nominal ledger vs. daybooks

The **nominal ledger** is a big book holding all of the financial information of a business. Therefore, a mistake in the nominal ledger could prove quite tricky to rectify. It seemed a better idea to record the information somewhere else, before putting it into the ledger.

It's always better for processes to have several stages, so that we can review our work as we go along, and that's exactly the idea behind the original bookkeeping process.

So, instead of writing transactions straight into the nominal ledger, accountants used to use smaller books to record transactions as they happened. These smaller books were, and are still, known as **daybooks**.

After **information** had been **recorded in** these **daybooks**, accountants would then check it for errors and **transfer it to the correct accounts in the nominal ledger.**

Other ledgers

Accountants also used to use **separate ledgers to figure out how much they owed to their suppliers and how much they were owed by their customers.** These types of ledgers are known as the **purchases ledger** and the **sales ledger**.

Trial balance

At the end of a certain period, for example a year, accountants would use all of the information from the nominal ledger to create a trial balance (a statement of all a business's debits and credits).

A trial balance helps a business make sure that all transactions have been correctly recorded, before they go on to create their financial statements.

The bookkeeping process

The financial statements are the end result of the bookkeeping process. Have a look at the diagram below to visualise this process:

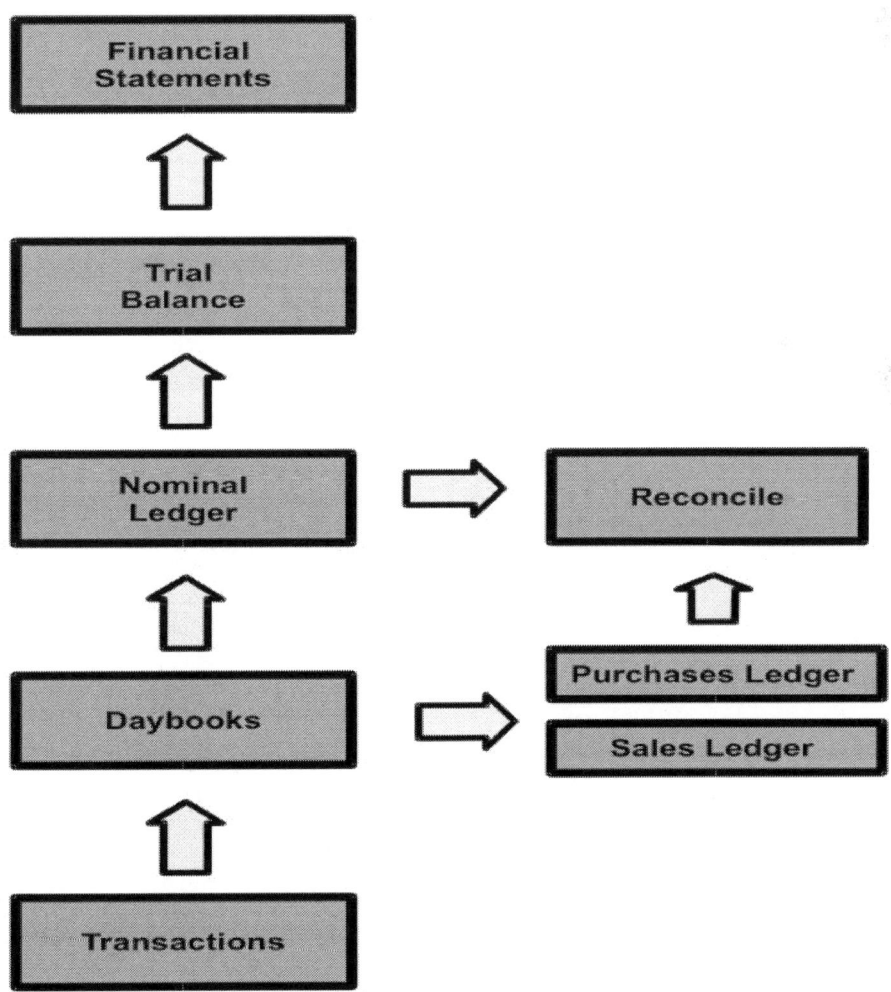

astranti
financial training

It's important that you understand this process. Even though accountants don't perform this process manually in the modern workplace, computerised accounting systems still run on these principles.

Transactions go from the daybooks to the nominal ledger. The nominal ledger is used to construct the trial balance and check for errors. Accountants then use the trial balance to construct the financial statements.

The sales ledger and the purchase ledger function **outside of this system**. They simply help businesses to better understand how much they owe or are owed to external parties and act as a useful double check, because if both the nominal ledger and sales/purchase ledgers agree then we're likely to have completed both correctly.

2.   Books of prime entry

Let's have a look at that diagram again to see which stage in the accounting process we are currently looking at:

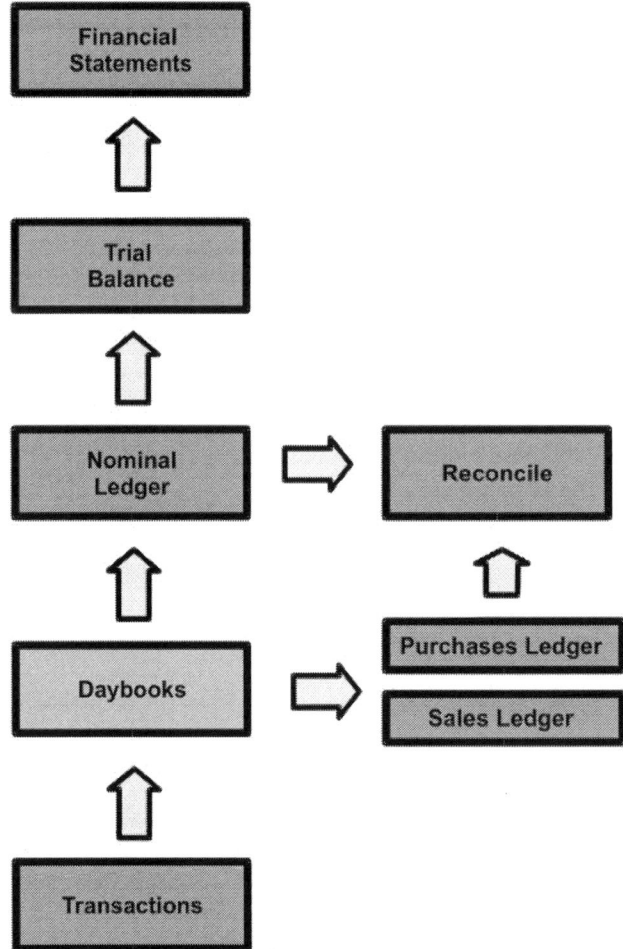

As we can see from the diagram, the **daybooks are the first place that transactions get recorded**.

'Books of prime entry' and 'journals' are other names for the daybooks.

Let's imagine a large clothing wholesaler, Carly's Clothes Ltd, that doesn't use an automated system of bookkeeping. Of course, this is unlikely to be the case nowadays, but for the purposes of understanding the method involved in keeping daybooks, let's suspend our disbelief.

Let's say Carly's Clothes has warehouses all over the UK. Every day, each warehouse sells thousands of items of clothing. It would be extremely difficult for all of these sales to be recorded directly into the nominal ledger as they occur every day – not least because it would mean that every individual warehouse would have to have an accountant on-hand to make the entries. A method of getting around this problem is to use 'books of prime entry' to record these transactions as they occur.

So, let's say Carly's Clothes has a warehouse in Manchester. Because Carly's Clothes Ltd is a wholesaler, they sell to a lot of other businesses and so make sales on credit – the customer (local clothing retailers) usually pay Carly within 30 days.

Every time a sale is made from Carly's Clothes' Manchester outlet on credit, an employee at the store records the sale in a book of prime entry used to hold information on all the credit sales transactions of the store. This kind of book of prime entry is referred to as a 'sales daybook'.

Notice how the sales daybook is only used to record credit sales. This is because a different daybook is used to record all cash transactions. This book is called the cashbook.

So, Carly's Clothes' Manchester warehouse records all of the information on sales in the sales daybook. **At the end of a certain period** (let's say a week),the information from the Manchester sales daybook can be **totalled up and entered into an account called 'the sales control account' in the nominal ledger**.

When using day books, businesses classify their monetary transactions into groups (such as sales, purchases, receipts of cash and payments) and they keep separate day books for each of these categories.

The groups into which the books of prime entry are usually split are shown in the following table:

Book of prime entry	What it records	For instance
Sales day book	Goods sold to customers on credit	Carly's Clothes Manchester sells a customer £1,000 of clothes on credit
Purchases day book	Goods purchased from suppliers on credit	Carly's Clothes Manchester purchases £3,000 of inventory on credit
Returns inwards day book	Returns of goods sold	A customer returns clothes worth £100 to Carly's Clothes Manchester
Returns outward day book	Returns of good purchased	Carly's Clothes Manchester has to return a proportion of inventory
Cash book	Money going in and out of the bank	Sales or purchases made in cash or from the company bank
Petty cash book	Small cash payments	The manager of Carly's Clothes Manchester store buys a birthday card for a member of staff from the department and uses the petty cash for this
Journal	'Unusual' items or error fixing	Carly's Clothes Manchester 'write-off' a bad debt from a customer who they know will never pay (unusual item)

Recording transactions in the daybooks

Example

The best way to learn about the books of prime entry is to go through an example of how a business would record its transactions into the books of prime entry.

Below is a list of transactions which Carly's Clothes' Manchester warehouse has been involved in over a period of a few days. These need adding to the day books.

(Note: In this example, PQ, LM, NO, RS, TU are external businesses).

01st Aug	Purchase goods from PQ costing **£800 on credit**
	Sold goods to LM for **£500 on credit**
02nd Aug	Sold goods to NO for **£100 on credit**
	Returned good to supplier PQ costing **£75**
03rd Aug	Purchased goods from RS costing **£250 on credit**
04th Aug	LM returns goods of **£300**
05th Aug	Sold good to TU costing **£150 on credit**
	TU returns goods of **£50**

Each of the transactions is also subject to the standard **20% UK sales tax which is not included in the above figures.**

Let's look at how we record these transactions in the store's books of prime entry:

So, first of all we have the goods purchased from PQ. Because this is a purchase and it is also a transaction made on credit, we record it in the purchases daybook rather than the cash book.

It will look like this:

Date	Doc. no.	Details	Value (£)	Sales tax(£)	Total (£)
		Purchases Daybook			
01/08	001	PQ	800	160	960

So, here we have the transaction recorded in the purchases daybook, with the value of sales tax added on. The transaction is also dated, with the details of the transaction being the initials of the party that the company purchased from.

Below is a representation of how all of these transactions will look when entered into the daybooks:

Date	Doc. no.	Details	Value (£)	Sales tax(£)	Total (£)
		Purchases Daybook			
01/08	001	PQ	800	160	960
03/08	002	RS	250	50	300
			1,050	**210**	**1,260**
		Sales Daybook			
01/08	101	LM	500	100	600
02/08	102	NO	100	20	120
05/08	103	TU	150	30	180
			750	**150**	**900**
		Return Inwards Daybook			
04/08	201	LM	300	60	360
05/08	202	TU	50	10	60
			350	**70**	**420**
		Returns Outwards Daybook			
02/08	2001	PQ	75	15	90

So, as you can see, the transactions have been recorded in the day books, along with their sales tax amounts. Pretty easy, really!

If you're wondering what the numbers in the document number column or the letters in the details column refer to, these numbers and letters form part of the coding system used to link the day books to the ledger. Let's learn more about this.

Coding

Each business uses their own coding system to label entries that they make in their daybooks, so that when the entries are transferred to the ledger, they can easily be traced back to their location in the daybooks.

So, in our example daybook entries, the numbers shown in the document number column are the codes used by Carly's Clothes Manchester.

In this particular example, '001' refers to the first entry made into one day book, '101' refers to the first entry made into another, '201' refers to the first entry made into yet another day book, and so on.

Businesses will use their own codes, which may vary from this method of coding. The coding system here is just an example of how daybook codes could work.

Similarly, the 'details column' in our daybook example shows the initials of the customer or business that each particular transaction relates to. For example 'PQ' refers to a transaction involving a supplier called Pants Quarter Ltd.

This code helps accountants to connect the transactions to the external suppliers or customers.

This is helpful for when accountants are using the sales ledger or the purchases ledger to work out how much they owe or are owed by different parties.

Again, this is just an example of what a coding system might look like, but all businesses will have their own systems which may vary.

The system will depend on how the company is organised, but any **good coding system should have the following aspects:**

- **Meaningful** – it helps if the coding has purpose and is useful. e.g. customer codes start with a C and supplier codes with an S so that it's immediately obvious what the code represents.

- **Unique** – an item should have only one possible code, e.g. customer A is C00001, customer B is C00002, and so on.

- **Clear** – coding should make the system more efficient, not more confusing! e.g. It would be unclear if Customer A's code is G8D£ and customer B's code is J3!A so there is no obvious link or relationship.

- **Standard size** – if a code needs to be 5 characters, then all codes should be 5 characters.

- **Self-checking** – codes can be checked because they are in a certain pattern e.g. All customer codes are one letter followed by 3 numbers and so any code entered which is not of that format can be rejected.

- **Future-proof** – codes should be designed with future coding in mind. e.g. A company starts coding its invoices with a C and 3 numbers and after two years when it gets to customer number 999 finds it needs to update the coding system. A little forethought might have meant starting with a C and 5 numbers as that would have ensured enough numbers for many years to come!

- **Compact** – a code should be as short as possible without missing important information. This needs to be balanced against future-proof of course. In our example a 3 digit code was short but not future proof, whereas an 8 digit code would be unnecessarily long.

3.   Purchases and sales ledgers

Let's look back at our diagram to figure out where we are in the accounting process now:

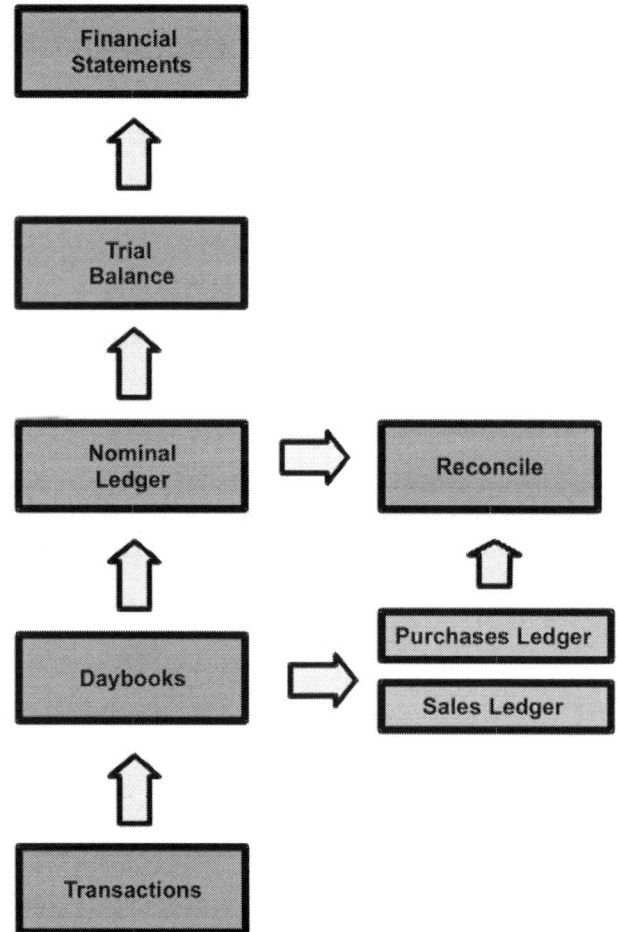

So, we have the sales, purchases and returns nicely recorded in the daybooks of Carly's Clothes Manchester. All of the transactions that we have seen Carly's Clothes involved in so far have been on credit – that means that the amounts are yet to be paid or received by the company. As we can see, the company frequently deals with many of the same businesses – both as customers and as suppliers.

It might be a good idea for Carly's Clothes to keep a record of how much they owe or are owed by each individual company, right?

Well, that's exactly what the sales and purchases ledgers are for!

In the sales and purchases ledger, businesses have accounts for each individual company and customer that they deal with.

Remember: these ledgers are used to keep track of credit purchases and sales, rather than cash purchases and sales. Cash transactions are dealt with in the cash book and transferred directly to the nominal ledger from there. We will have a look at the cash book in more detail in just a second.

We can use the information we have from Carly's Clothes' daybooks to demonstrate what the purchases ledger and the sales ledger would look like for the company.

Purchases ledger

In the purchases day book, the first purchase that has been recorded is a purchase worth £960 from a supplier with the initials PQ (Pants Quarter).

So, this would get recorded in the PQ account, inside the purchases ledger, like this:

Date	Details	£	Date	Details	£
			Purchases Ledger		
			PQ		
			01st Aug	001	960

As you can see, this amount has been recorded on the credit side. That is because **this account is a supplier account and therefore represents payables, which are liabilities.**

According to DEADCLIC, **we always credit an increase in liabilities** (dead **CL**ic). Therefore, this transaction is credited to the PQ account. This ledger operates in the same way as the purchase ledger control (payables) account in the nominal ledger, which is covered later in the chapter.

In the 'details' column, we have a reference to where this particular transaction can be found in the daybooks, as explained earlier, 001 represents the first entry in a the purchases daybook.

Now, **unlike the nominal ledger, the purchases and sales ledgers are NOT subject to double entry**. They use a system of debits and credits just as the nominal ledger does, but transactions do NOT need to be entered more than once.

So, the entry shown above is the ONLY entry we make for this transaction.

Now, we can see that Carly's Clothes Ltd returned £90 worth of clothes to PQ on the 02nd August. This too needs to be accounted for in the PQ account, like this:

Date	Details	£	Date	Details	£
		Purchases Ledger			
		PQ			
02nd Aug	2001	90	01st Aug	001	960

This is because **the amount represents a reduction in the amount that Carly's Clothes owe to PQ – it is a decrease in a liability and therefore should be recorded as a debit.**

These are the only two transactions between PQ and Carly's Clothes during the period, and therefore the account shown above is what the PQ account in the purchases ledger should look like.

So, the total amount that Carly's Clothes owe to Pants Quarter at the end of the period is:

£960 - £90 = £870

This will be the balance of the PQ account in the purchase ledger.

When all the transactions are put into the purchases ledger, it will look like this:

Date	Details	£	Date	Details	£
		Purchases Ledger			
		PQ			
02nd Aug	2001	90	01st Aug	001	960
		RS			
			03rd Aug	002	300

Sales ledger

Now let's have a look at how we record transactions in the sales ledger. The first transaction we have recorded in the sales day book is a sale of £600 to LM on 01st August. We record this in the LM account, like so:

Date	Details	£	Date	Details	£
		Sales Ledger			
		LM			
01st Aug	101	600			

Since this represents an increase in asset it is debited, keeping in line with DEADCLIC which specifies that we must debit an increase in assets (**DeA**d click). This ledger operates in the same way as the sales ledger control (receivables) account in the nominal ledger which will be covered later in this chapter.

On 4th August, Carly's Clothes also received returns of £360 from LM. This amount was recorded in the returns inwards daybook. We record this in the LM account in the sales ledger like so:

Date	Details	£	Date	Details	£
		Sales Ledger			
		LM			
01st Aug	101	600	04th Aug	201	360

So, the total amount that is owed to Carly's Clothes Ltd by LM is:

£600 - £360 = £240

Therefore, this is the balance of the LM income account at the end of the period.

When all the transactions from the daybooks have been entered into the sales ledger, it will look like this:

Date	Details	£	Date	Details	£
		Sales Ledger			
		LM			
01st Aug	101	600	04th Aug	201	360
		NO			
02nd Aug	102	120			
		TU			
05th Aug	103	180	05th Aug	202	60

4. Cash books

When a company makes a cash transaction – by which we mean a sale, purchase or other transaction that is made from the company's bank account – this gets recorded in the cash book.

Below is an example of what a non-integrated cash book would look like, using the examples given earlier from Carly's Clothes Ltd (imagining for a moment that these transactions were CASH transactions and not credit transactions):

		Cash Book			
Date	Details	Receipts	Payments	Discounts	Total
1st	101 (LM)	600			600
1st	001 (PQ)		960		960
2nd	102 (NO)	120			120
3rd	002 (RS)		300		300
Total		**720**	**1,160**		**1,880**

As you can see, the cash book is just a list of transactions ordered by date, according to whether they are receipts or payments. Note that there is a column too for discounts, had any discounts been paid or received.

astranti
financial training

At the end of a period of time (e.g. a week) the totals can be transferred from here into the 'bank' account in the nominal ledger.

Petty cash book

Much like the cash book, we use the petty cash book to record transactions of money, the only difference being that **it generally only records small transactions usually made in cash.**

The petty cash book works on an 'imprest system'.

This just means that the person in charge of the petty cash book is given a pre-determined balance (imprest) for a period, and must make all necessary transactions using that set balance. At the end of the period, this imprest amount is topped up from the bank account.

Petty cash payments are evidenced with receipts called petty cash vouchers, which are signed by the person who receives the cash.

The layout of the book is columnar just like the cash book. We record payments in the petty cash book in exactly the same way, the only difference being that petty cash, as the name suggests, deals with much smaller sums of money paid from cash rather than the bank.

5. From daybooks to the nominal ledger

After the daybooks have been completed for a period of time (e.g. a week), transactions are totalled up and recorded in the nominal ledger. Let's remind ourselves of where we now are in the bookkeeping process by looking at the diagram again:

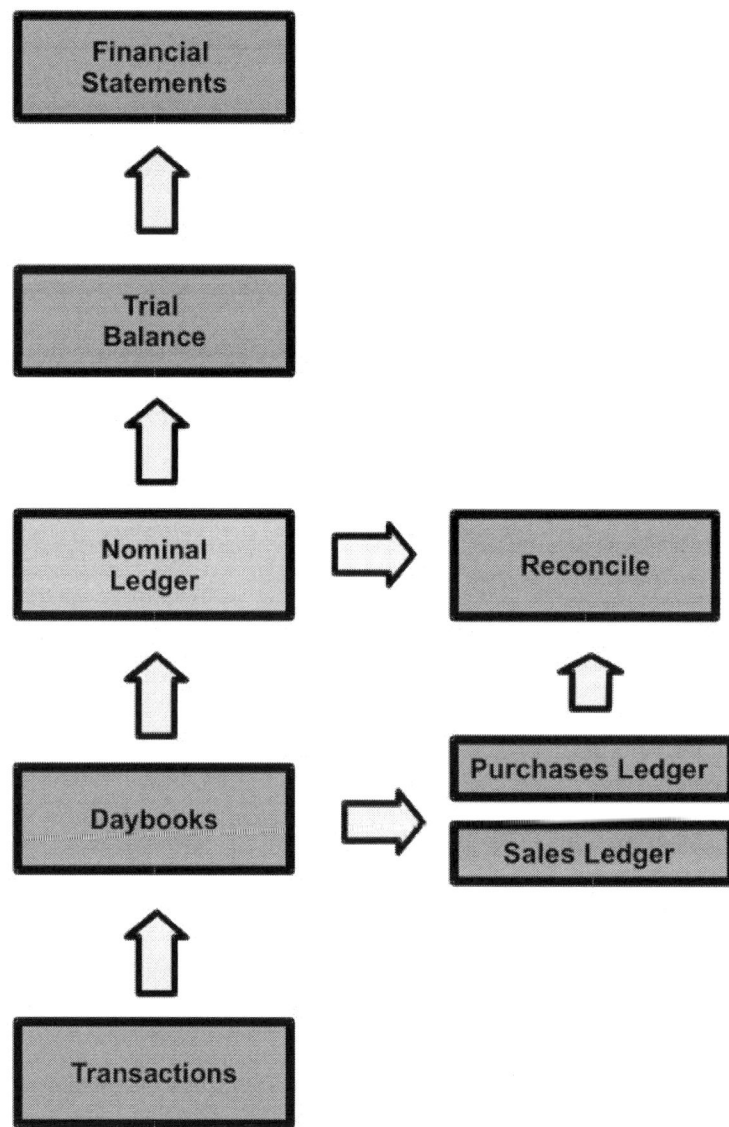

So, we've entered the transactions into the daybooks and those transactions have been entered into the sales and purchases ledgers too. As well as entering information into the sales and purchases ledgers, we also put it into the nominal ledger.

Let's return to Carly's Clothes Manchester. As we have seen, they have successfully recorded all of the store's transactions into the books of prime entry for the period, and they look like this:

Date	Doc. no.	Details	Value (£)	Sales tax (£)	Total (£)
Purchases Daybook					
01/08	001	PQ	800	160	960
03/08	002	RS	250	50	300
			1,050	210	1,260
Sales Daybook					
01/08	101	LM	500	100	600
02/08	102	NO	100	20	120
05/08	103	TU	150	30	180
			750	150	900
Return Inwards Daybook					
04/08	201	LM	300	60	360
05/08	202	TU	50	10	60
			350	70	420
Returns Outwards Daybook					
02/08	2001	PQ	75	15	90

The nominal ledger works on a system of double entry. So, when moving the transactions across from the daybooks, we need to remember to record both aspects of each transaction.

Now, using these same transactions, we will now look at how we integrate all of this information into the ledger, making sure we debit and credit each account correctly.

We know from the information that we have that during August, Carly's Clothes made sales of £900 on credit (including tax):

£600 + £120 + £180 = £900. Of that £900, £150 was tax.

The last sale was made on 05th Aug, so we can take this as the date that the total was found.

So, let's see how this gets from the daybooks to the nominal ledger.

Sales and receivables

Sales, tax and receivables

Date	£	Date	£
		Sales	
		05th Aug Receivables	750
		Tax	
		05th Aug Receivables	150
		Receivables (Sales ledger control account)	
05th Aug Sales	750		
Tax	150		

The receivables account (also known as the sales ledger control account) and the payables account (also known as the purchase ledger control account) contain all the information on amounts owed by customers and to suppliers.

We know that Carly's Clothes Ltd made a total of £750 credit sales. Because this is a control account, we do not need to show every individual transaction, we simply show the total of all transactions. Sales is a credit because it is income (dead **CIIc**)

The £150 tax is a credit because it is a liability as it is money owed to the tax authorities (dead **CLic**)

The receivables account is an asset account, and as we can see an increase in assets is always DEBITED (**DeAd** clic). £900 is owed from customers.

Returns inwards

Let's now deal with the entries in the returns inwards daybook.

The returns inwards daybook shows all returns made to the business by customers. The total amount recorded in the returns inwards daybook for the period is:

£360 + £60 = £420. Of these returns £70 relates to tax.

As with sales, the last return inwards was made on 05th Aug, so we can take this as the date that the total was found.

astranti
financial training

Now, because we are talking about the return of items that have been bought on credit, we can assume that when the items were returned, none of the payment had actually been received by Carly's Clothes yet.

Therefore, the returns represent a DECREASE in receivables (a credit) – because the business is no longer going to receive money for those items, and a reversal of a sale (a debit).

Recording this amount in the ledger therefore looks like this:

Date		£	Date		£
		Sales			
05th Aug	Receivables	350	05th Aug	Receivables	750
		Tax			
05th Aug	Receivables	70	05th Aug	Receivables	150
		Receivables (Sales ledger control account)			
05th Aug	Sales	750	05th Aug	Sales	350
05th Aug	Tax	150	05th Aug	Tax	70

Returns inwards are accounted for in the opposite way to sales, since they represent the returns of goods that have been sold and therefore are the reverse of sales transactions.

Purchase expenses and payables

So, we've accounted for the sales. But what about the purchases? Well, the process is very similar and easy to follow.

Purchase expenses, tax and payables

The total amount of credit purchases made in the period including tax was:

£960 + £300 = £1,260. Tax on this was £210.

Purchases of stock or inventory are costs involved in keeping the business running – these items are either sold on, or made into other products which are sold on. These are called **purchase expenses** (or just purchases). In accordance with DEADCLIC, an increase in expenses should always be debited (**DE**ad clic).

This amount also needs to be recorded in the purchase ledger control(payables) account in the nominal ledger. This account shows the liabilities that a company owes to suppliers. An increase in liabilities should always be credited (dead **CLic**).

Date		£	Date		£
Purchase expenses (purchases)					
05th Aug	Payables	1,050			
Tax					
05th Aug	Payables	210			
Payables (Purchase ledger control account)					
			05th Aug	Purchase expenses	1,050
			05th Aug	Tax	210

Returns outward

Now it's time to look at the returns outwards daybook. Returns outwards represent returns that Carly's Clothes Ltd has made to its suppliers and so they are the reverse of the above transactions.

As we can see, Carly's Clothes Ltd only made one return, worth £90, on the 02nd August. Tax on this was £15. So, because the company's purchases were made on credit, we can assume that by the time the return was made before the balance was paid, so the return of goods to suppliers results in a reduction of payables for Carly's Clothes Ltd.

Date		£	Date		£
Purchase expenses					
05th Aug	Payables	1,050	05th Aug	Payables	75
Tax					
05th Aug	Payables	210	05th Aug	Payables	15
Payables (Purchase ledger control account)					
05th Aug	Expenses	75	05th Aug	Purchase expenses	1,050
05th Aug	Tax	15	05th Aug	Tax	210

Of course, sales and purchases of goods by a business will also affect the inventory account (the stock held for sale) and the double entry for that will also need to be recorded in the nominal ledger – something we'll cover in a later chapter.

6. Reconciliation

Let's have another look at our accounting process diagram.

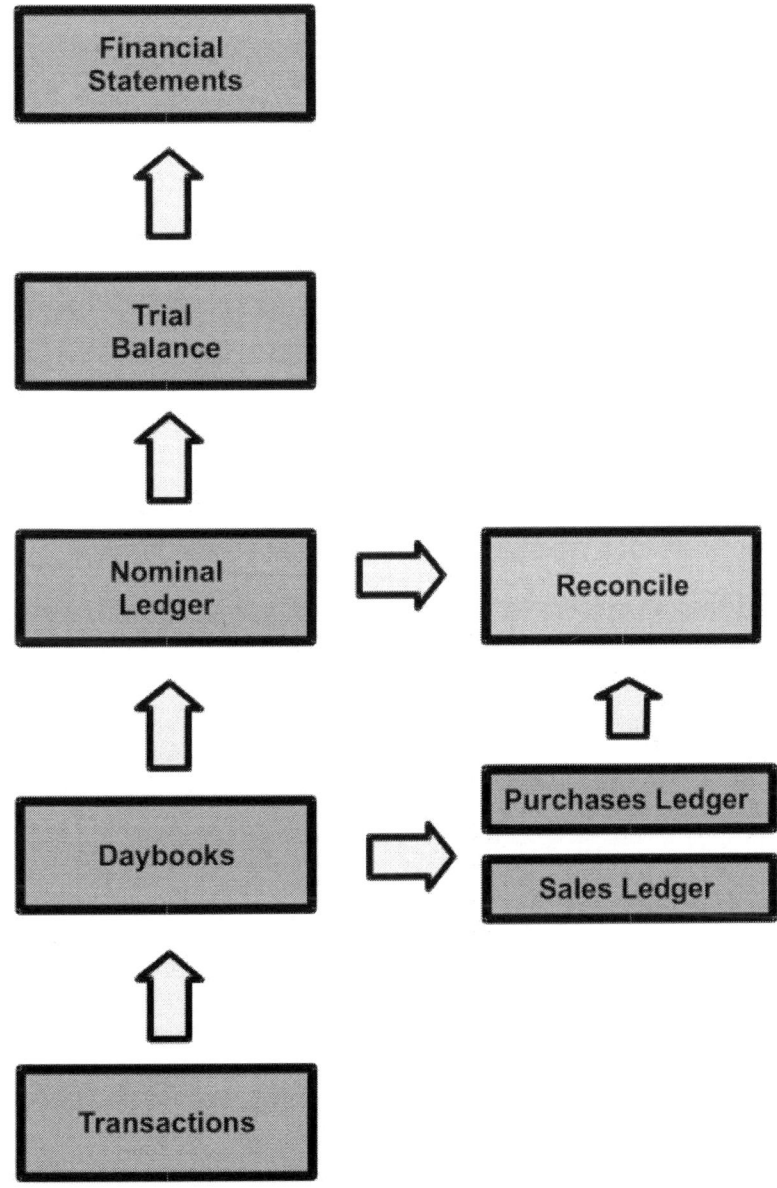

As we can see, there is a step here called 'reconcile' - which refers to the fact that the purchases and sales ledgers can be reconciled with the nominal ledger to confirm that transactions have been recorded correctly.

If we take our sales ledger for instance:

Date	Details	£	Date	Details	£
		Sales Ledger			
		LM			
01st Aug	101	600	04th Aug	201	360
		NO			
02nd Aug	102	120			
		TU			
05th Aug	103	180	05th Aug	202	60
Total		**900**			**420**

We can see that the balance on our sales ledger is £900 - £420 = £480.

That should equal the amount owed by customers i.e. the receivables balance in the nominal ledger account. Let's check!

Receivables (Sales ledger control account)					
05th Aug	Sales	750	05th Aug	Sales	350
05th Aug	Tax	150	05th Aug	Tax	70
Total		**900**			**420**

And yes – the total due from customers is £900 - £420 = £480.

OK, when just doing a few transactions like this it was easy! However, if a company has millions of transactions in a period there's a lot of room for error and the fact that the sales ledger and receivables account in the nominal ledger reconcile provides a lot of assurance that a mistake hasn't been made.

Trial balance and the financial statements

You'll notice from the diagram that the next stages of the process are to undertake a trial balance and from that produce financial statements. We'll examine those next steps in the next chapter.

astranti
financial training

CIMA BA3 Study Text

Chapter 4

Producing a Trial Balance and Financial Statements

1. Balancing the books

You've probably heard the phrase, 'balancing the books'. When thinking about this, it's not hard to envision dusty, hard-backed books balanced on scales!

Well, when balancing the books we are not trying to make sure the financial books literally weigh the same, but we are trying to ensure that our financial information is equal in a different way; that **the credits add up to the same amount as the debits!**

This ensures that all of the money involved in each transaction is accounted for. If you've ever heard of money disappearing, it was probably because of faulty account balancing!

Creating a trial balance

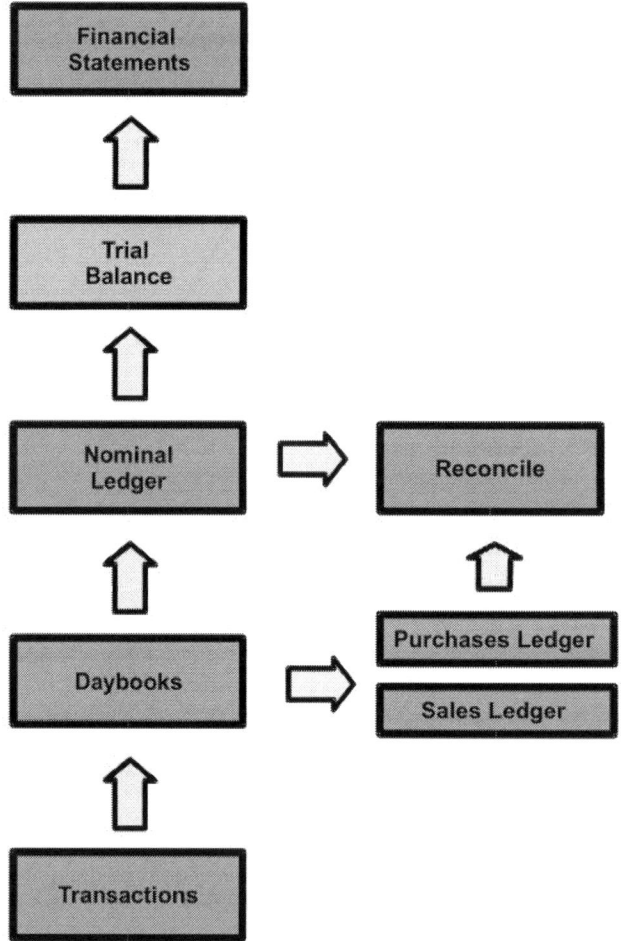

Our goal in this chapter is to undertake the next stage in our process towards producing financial statements – producing a trial balance. As you can see, the trial balance flows on directly from the nominal ledger accounts that we produced in earlier chapters.

We'll start by setting out an example that we'll use to demonstrate the process of creating a trial balance throughout this chapter.

Example

The following ledger is taken from Louie's Pizza Place, a fast food restaurant in New York City.

Date			$'000's				$'000's
		Building					
01st Sept	Balance b/f		98				
		Inventory					
01st Sept	Balance b/f		7				
		Receivables					
01st Sept	Balance b/f		2				
		Cash in bank					
01st Sept	Balance b/f		15				
		Loan					
				01st Sept	Balance b/f		50
		Payables					
				01st Sept	Balance b/f		12
		Capital					
				01st Sept	Balance b/f		60

Note: 'Balance b/f' simply means balance brought forward from a previous period. Because T-accounts record transactions over time, we need to know where the starting balances come from when we start a new ledger.

So, now we have our starting information, we want to record the transactions made in a period and make sure both the credit and the debit sides add up to the same number.

2.   Entering the transactions

Here are all the transactions Louie was involved in during the first week of September:

01ˢᵗ Sept: Louie bought **$2,000** of inventory using cash.

02ⁿᵈ Sept: Louie sells **$1,500** worth of inventory for **$11,500** cash.

03ʳᵈ Sept: He received **$500** interest from his bank.

05ᵗʰ Sept: Louie pays off **$2,000** of a loan with money from the bank.

06ᵗʰ Sept: Louie pays wages to employees, coming to **$6,500**.

07ᵗʰ Sept: Louie pays **$1,000** for electric and heating bills.

This should be a non-current asset rather than an expense.

So, for each transaction Louie makes, we make a record of which account the money is credited from, and to which account the money is debited to. So, for example:

01ˢᵗ Sept: Louie bought **$2,000** of inventory.

These transaction are broken down in the following way:

Louie takes **$2,000** from his bank account to pay for inventory. Withdrawing money from a bank account is a decrease in assets, which makes it a credit from the bank, which we record as follows:

	Bank			
01ˢᵗ Sept	Balance b/f	$15,000	**01ˢᵗ Sept** Purchase exp.	**$2,000**

But, he also needs to record the gaining of £2,000 worth of stock. Costs involved in keeping a business running are expenses and as Louie is buying stock, we debit the purchases expense account to reflect this increase in inventory:

	Purchase expenses	
01ˢᵗ Sept	**Cash in bank**	**$2,000**

So now, the $2,000 Louie spent on stock has now been properly recorded on both sides, as a credit to his bank account, and a debit to his purchase expenses. In the nominal ledger remember that for every debit there is an equal and opposite credit.

Let's have a look at the transactions on 02ⁿᵈ September. Firstly, Louie sells **$1,500** worth of inventory for **$11,500**. The revenue from this sale is accounted for as follows:

Bank

01ˢᵗ Sept	Balance b/f	$15,000	01ˢᵗ Sept	Purchase exp.	$2,000
02ⁿᵈ Sept	**Sales**	**$11,500**			

Sales

		01ˢᵗ Sept	Bank	**$11,500**

So, we can see that the $11,500 revenue has been debited to the company bank account, since the bank account is an asset account (**DeAd clic**) and the sale indicates an increase in income which is a credit (dead **ClIc**).

I'm sure that you can see by now – whenever an account is debited or credited, the details given in the description of the T account need to refer to the account that the opposite side of the transaction can be found in.

For example, with this profit amount, we debit the bank account with $11,500, with the reference 'sales', and we credit the sales account with $11,500, with the reference 'bank'.

We also need to make a note that $1,500 worth of inventory has been sold. The inventory account in the nominal ledger only deals with opening and closing inventory balances. It doesn't record sales or purchases of inventory within a set accounting period.

Therefore **no T-accounts are required for the sale of inventory at this point** in our example. We will return to inventory account and detail how to record the opening and closing balances in it, at a later point.

Remaining transactions

Let's have a look at all of the transactions entered into Louis' ledger.

When Louis records all of the transactions in each of the accounts, he ends up with a ledger account that looks like this:

Date		$'000's	Date		$'000's
		Building			
01ˢᵗ Sept	Balance b/f	98			
		Inventories			
01ˢᵗ Sept	Balance b/f	7			

astranti financial training

Purchase expense

01st Sept	Bank	2			

Receivables

01st Sept	Balance b/f	2			

Bank

01st Sept	Balance b/f	15	01st Sept	Purchase exp.	2
02nd Sept	Sales	11.5	05th Sept	Loan	2
03rd Sept	Interest	0.5	06th Sept	Admin expenses	6.5
			07th Sept	Admin expenses	1

Sales

		02nd Bank		11.5

Other income (interest earned)

		03rd Sept	Bank	0.5

Loan

05th Sept	Bank	2	01st Sept	Balance b/f	50

Payables

		01st Sept	Balance b/f	12

Admin expenses

06th Sept	Bank	6.5			
07th Sept	Bank	1			

Capital

		01st Sept	Balance b/f	60

(Note: the expenses here refer to the $6,500 in wages paid to employees and the $1,000 in electricity and heating bills).

Since every transaction has now been recorded, **we can actually see that we've done all our debits and credits in full because both sides add up to the same number:**

All debits: $98 + 7 + 2 + 2 + 15 + 11.5 + 0.5 + 2 + 6.5 + 1 = $ **145.5**

All credits: $2 + 2 + 6.5 + 1 + 11.5 + 0.5 + 50 + 12 + 60 = $ **145.5**

3. Balancing asset accounts

At the end of a period of time, say a month or a year, the various nominal ledger accounts are summarised and balanced.

The first step in the end of period process is to balance off the asset accounts and then calculate the balance to be carried forward to the next period. It is a very simple process.

So, let's use the bank account from the ledger and follow the 5 steps it takes to balance an account.

Here's the account again:

Bank					
01st Sept	Balance b/f	15	01st Sept	Purchase exp.	2
02nd Sept	Sales	11.5	05th Sept	Loan	2
03rd Sept	Interest	0.5	06th Sept	Admin expenses	6.5
			07th Sept	Admin expenses	1

Step 1: Calculate the balance

Bank					
01st Sept	Balance b/f	15	01st Sept	Purchase exp.	2
02nd Sept	Sales	11.5	05th Sept	Loan	2
03rd Sept	Interest	0.5	06th Sept	Admin expenses	6.5
			07th Sept	Admin expenses	1

The balance is the total debits minus the total credits.

Debits:

$15 + 11.5 + 0.5 = 27$

Credits:

$2 + 2 + 6.5 + 1 = 11.5$

Debits less credits:

$27 - 11.5 = 15.5$

So the balance is **$15,500**.

Step 2: Enter the balance carried down to make both sides balance

Bank					
01st Sept	Balance b/f	15	01st Sept	Purchase exp.	2
02nd Sept	Sales	11.5	05th Sept	Loan	2
03rd Sept	Interest	0.5	06th Sept	Admin expenses	6.5
			07th Sept	Admin expenses	1
			30th Sept	**Balance c/d**	**15.5**

So, the cash in bank had a debit (positive) balance of $15,500. Therefore, we enter the sum on the credit side to make the account balance.

Step 3: Total up each side

Bank					
01st Sept	Balance b/f	15	01st Sept	Purchase exp.	2
02nd Sept	Sales	11.5	05th Sept	Loan	2
03rd Sept	Interest	0.5	06th Sept	Admin expenses	6.5
			07th Sept	Admin expenses	1
			30th Sept	Balance c/d	15.5
		27			**27**

They should be the same if you calculated the balance correctly.

Step 4: Enter the balance brought down

		Bank			
01st Sept	Balance b/f	15	01st Sept	Purchase exp.	2
02nd Sept	Sales	11.5	05th Sept	Loan	2
03rd Sept	Interest	0.5	06th Sept	Admin expenses	6.5
			07th Sept	Admin expenses	1
			30th Sept	Balance c/d	15.5
		27			27
	Balance b/d	**15.5**			

The balance b/d is the balance to be taken forward to the next set of accounts – in this case the next month.

Step 5: Make sure all debits are assets and all credits are liabilities or capital

Well, cash in the bank is an asset, and therefore in this case it is recorded on the debit side, since it is a positive amount, it shows the amount of money left in the bank.

Had the bank balance been negative, it would have been a debt (liability), because this would have been an amount of money the company owed the bank, and thus a credit in the account.

This last step is just a check that no silly errors have been made.

Balancing the other accounts

Assuming no other transactions in the month, let's balance all the other accounts too.

Date		$'000's	Date		$'000's
Building					
1ˢᵗ Sept	Balance b/f	98	31ˢᵗ Sept	Balance c/d	98
		98			98
31ˢᵗ Sept	Balance b/d	98			
Receivables					
1ˢᵗ Sept	Balance b/f	2	31ˢᵗ Sept	Balance c/d	2
		2			2
31ˢᵗ Sept	Balance b/d	2			
Loan					
31ˢᵗ Sept	Bank	2	1ˢᵗ Sept	Balance b/f	50
31ˢᵗ Sept	Balance c/d	48			
		50			50
			31ˢᵗ Sept	Balance c/d	48
Payables					
31ˢᵗ Sept	Balance c/d	12	01ˢᵗ Sept	Balance b/f	12
		12			12
			31ˢᵗ Sept	Balance c/d	12

The capital account is done slightly differently. Capital is money owed to shareholders, and as a profit or loss has been made in this period, there's now more or less capital. We'll deal with this later, but for the time being here it as a reminder.

			Date		$'000's
Capital					
			01ˢᵗ Sept	Balance b/f	60

4.   Totalling the income and expense accounts

Income and expense accounts are treated slightly differently from asset or liability accounts. We are going to use these later to create the income statement, from which we'll conclude whether a profit or a loss has been made.

Income and expense accounts do not have balances to be carried forward to the next accounting period though, they relate just to this period. Sales this year are just that – sales this year – they don't carry forward to sales next year, or the year after that.

At this stage we simply add up the totals of the income and expense accounts. Let's do that now by taking all the income and expense accounts from our set of accounts and adding up the totals.

Date	$'000's	Date	$'000's
Purchase expenses			
01st Sept Bank	2		
	2		
Sales			
		02nd Sept Bank	11.5
			11.5
Other income (interest earned)			
		03rd Sept Bank	0.5
			0.5
Admin expenses			
06th Sept Bank	6.5		
07th Sept Bank	1		
	7.5		

Cost of sales and inventory

The cost of sales is, as the description sounds, the costs of the items sold in the period.

In our example, if you look back at the question, it tells us that there were sales of $11,500, of items which cost $1,500 to purchase. The $1,500 is the 'cost' of the 'sales' made.

Unfortunately most situations involve many sale items without any clear record of exactly how much each cost. As a result the cost of sales is calculated as follows:

Opening inventories	7.0
Purchases	2.0
	9.0
Closing inventories	(7.5)
	(1.5)

We started the period with $7,000 of stock, and purchased another $2,000, meaning we had £9,000 of items available to sell in total. By the end of the period we measured closing inventory to be $7,500, meaning we must have sold stock worth $1,500 during the period.

We can also see these same items in the cost of sales T account

Cost of sales

01st Sept	Inventory	$7,000	01st Sept	Balance	$1,500
30th Sept	Purchase exp.	$2,000	30th Sept	Inventory	$7,500
		$9,000			$9,000

The final balance is also $1,500.

We need to put the other sides of the double entry in too:

Firstly the purchases account:

Purchase expenses

01st Sept	Bank	$2,000	30 Sept	Cost of sales	2,000
		$2,000			$2,000

This is now balanced, and so no more needs to be done for purchase expenses for this period.

Next let's consider inventory:

	Inventory				
01ˢᵗ Sept	Balance b/f	$7,000	01ˢᵗ Sept	Cost of sales	$7,000
30ᵗʰ Sept	Cost of sales	$7,500		Bal c/d	$7,500
		£14,500			£14,500
	Bal b/d	$7,500			

Effectively we take out the opening inventory at the start of the period (credit), and then add back the closing inventory at the end (debit) and then balance off the account.

As you might expect, the closing inventory is also the balance on the account at the end of the period.

5. Trial balance

What is a trial balance?

Making a financial statement straight from your accounts can be a complicated and frustrating business. Imagine if you took the figures from your account ledgers and put them into a financial statement only to find that the accounts weren't balanced. You would have to go back to the original ledgers and work out where the figures had gone wrong!

This is why, before you produce financial statements, it makes sense to first summarise the accounts. There are two main reasons for doing this:

- Firstly, producing a summary will **tell you whether your accounts are balanced** or not.

- Secondly, once you have a (balanced) summary of accounts, then it becomes **a lot simpler to take those figures and put them into the financial statement**.

This is the purpose of the trial balance. **A trial balance is, in effect, the total of the balanced and totalled ledger accounts.** What happens is that we take all the individual balanced accounts and totalled income and expense accounts and list them on a sheet, with debits on one side, and credits on the other.

Trial Balance of Louie's Pizza Place as of 31ˢᵗ September 20X1

Account	DR $'000	CR $'000
Bank	15.5	
Building	98	
Inventories	7.5	
Receivables	2	
Loan		48
Payables		12
Capital		60
Cost of sales	1.5	
Sales		11.5
Other income		0.5
Expenses	7.5	
Total	**132**	**132**

As you can see, both sides are equal, and so our trial balance is correct!

Or is it? It is balanced, but it not necessarily 'correct'.

Even when DR = CR, it is still possible for mistakes to have been made in the ledger, but the fact is has balanced gives us a lot of reassurance that transactions have been treated correctly.

6. The income statement

Income and expense accounts record transactions on a period by period basis e.g. month by month or year by year. Transactions are NOT carried forward at the end of the accounting period.

Instead, at the end of the period, they are closed off and emptied. **All the income and expense balances are taken to the income statement.**

Let's do that here starting with our cost of sales account. Here it was from our earlier working:

Cost of sales					
01ˢᵗ Sept	Inventory	$7,000	**01ˢᵗ Sept**	**Income statemt.**	**$1,500**
30ᵗʰ Sept	Purchase exp.	$2,000	30ᵗʰ Sept	Inventory	$7,500
		$9,000			$9,000

The balance is transferred to the income statement.

We repeat the same process for the other accounts, adding an entry on the opposite side of where the balance is to make the totals the same.

Date		$'000's	Date		$'000's
Sales					
31ˢᵗ Sept	**Income statemt.**	**11.5**	02ⁿᵈ Sept	Bank	11.5
		11.5			11.5
Other income (interest earned)					
30ᵗʰ Sept	**Income statemt.**	**0.5**	03ʳᵈ Sept	Bank	0.5
		0.5			0.5
Expenses					
06ᵗʰ Sept	Bank	6.5			
07ᵗʰ Sept	Bank	1	**30ᵗʰ Sept**	**Income statemt.**	**7.5**
		7.5			7.5

Of course we need another side to those new double entries, and that is the income statement (also called the profit and loss account).

Income statement					
30ᵗʰ Sept	Cost of sales	1.5	30ᵗʰ Sept	Sales	11.5
30ᵗʰ Sept	Expenses	7.5	30ᵗʰ Sept	Other income	0.5
	Profit (to capital)	**3.0**			
		12.0			12.0

So, we've posted each of the other sides of the double entry to the income statement. **The difference between the two sides is then the profit** (if it's on the debit side) **or a loss** (if it's on the credit side). In this case there's a £3,000 profit.

Transferring income to the capital account

The capital account represents money owed to the owners or shareholders. As a profit was made during the month, that's more money due to the shareholders.

At the end of the period, the total profit is transferred out of the income statement account to the capital account.

The capital account will therefore look like this:

	Capital			
		01st Sept	Balance b/f	60
31st Sept	Balance c/d	63	31st Sept Income statemt.	3
		63		63
			31st Sept Balance b/d	63

Just to check we've done this right we can update our trial balance, taking out the income and expenses accounts and adding in the new capital account balance.

Revised Trial Balance of Louie's Pizza Place as of 31st September 20X1

Account	DR $'000	CR $'000
Bank	15.5	
Building	98	
Inventories	7.5	
Receivables	2	
Loan		48
Payables		12
Capital		63
Total	**123**	**123**

That all balances nicely, so that's correct.

7. Financial statements

On our journey to take all the transactions of the business and create a set of financial statements to present to shareholders and other stakeholders of the business, we are nearing the end!

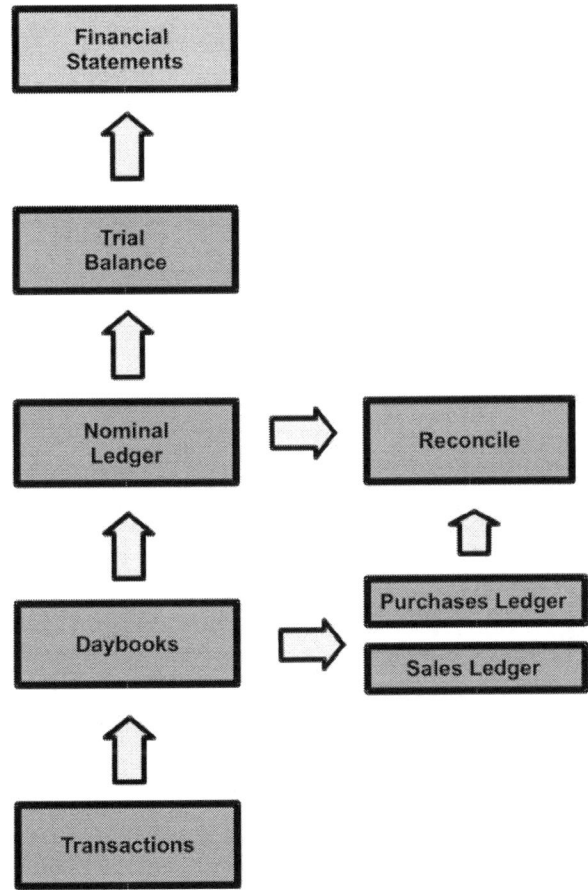

We have a final trial balance, and a statement of profit or loss, and from these we can create the financial statements.

astranti
financial training

The income statement

The income statement calculates the profit or loss that a business makes in a given period by subtracting the cost of sales and expenses from the income, giving us the profit or loss.

The income statement can be derived from the related nominal ledger account. Here is our example from earlier as a reminder:

Date		$'000's	Date		$'000's
	Income statement				
30th Sept	Cost of sales	1.5	30th Sept	Sales	11.5
30th Sept	Expenses	7.5	30th Sept	Other income	0.5
	Profit (to capital)	3.0			
		12.0			12.0

From this we simply sum this up in a table to create an income statement like this:

Income Statement - Louie's Pizza Place for the month ending 31st September 20X1

	$'000's
Sales	11.5
Less: Cost of sales	(1.5)
Gross profit	**10.0**
Add: Other income	0.5
Less: Expenses	(7.5)
Net profit	**3.0**

The **gross profit line shows the profit directly made in making and selling the product or service** – in this case pizzas and other food and drink items.

The **net profit is the profit after all other income and expenses are taken off.**

The trading account

Within the income statement, the top half of the statement where the gross profit is shown can also be shown including inventory and purchases, in what is known as the trading account.

We touched on this area earlier when calculating our cost of sales using the inventory account. This is how the trading account looks when it sits in the top half of the income statement:

		$'000's	$'000's
Sales			11.5
Less:	Cost of sales		
	Opening inventories	7.0	
	Purchases	2.0	
		9.0	
	Closing inventories	(7.5)	
			(1.5)
Gross Profit			10.0

Statement of financial position

Using the principle behind the accounting equation (Assets = Equity + Liabilities), we can produce a document which lists all of a business' assets and all of their liabilities. This is called a statement of financial position.

This is quite easy to do at this stage because we can simply take the balance from our **final trial balance**, which showed the assets and liabilities of the business and **show them in a table form, organised by assets, liabilities and capital.**

Here was the trial balance for Louie's Pizza Place after closing off the books:

Account	DR $'000	CR $'000
Bank	15.5	
Building	98	
Inventories	7.5	
Receivables	2	
Loan		48
Payables		12
Capital		63
Total	**123**	**123**

These balances are then transferred to the statement of financial position:

Statement of Financial Position as at 31st September 20X1

	$'000's	$'000's
Assets		
Non-current assets:		
Building		98.0
Current assets:		
Inventories	7.5	
Receivables	2.0	
Bank	15.5	
		25.0
		123.0
Capital and liabilities		
Capital		
Capital b/f	60.0	
Net profit	3.0	
		63.0
Non-current liabilities:		
Loan		48.0
Current liabilities:		
Payables		12.0
		123.0

You will notice that the statement of financial position splits out both assets and liabilities into current and non-current. Current simply means that the asset or liability is due to be paid off within a year. Non-current is more than one year.

So, for example, the building is expected to last many years and so is non-current, whilst the inventories are expected to be sold within a year and so are current.

The balance sheet

You'll often hear the statement of financial position called the 'balance sheet'. This is because the top half and the bottom half should have the same total. The statement of financial position balancing is the **final test that all the transactions have been done correctly**. If it does not balance then there's an error somewhere that will need to be identified!

The Statement of Changes In Equity

The Statement of Changes in Equity shows the **changes** in the shareholder's **equity** over a period of time (often a year).

The statement shows the amount of equity at the beginning of a period, all the changes to that equity, and then the equity balance at the end of the period.

Here's the statement in changes in equity for Louie's Pizza Place:

	Share capital	Share premium	Retained Earnings	Total
	$'000's	$'000's	$'000's	$'000's
Balance b/f	20	10	30	60
Income for the period			3	3
Dividends paid				0
Balance c/f	**20**	**10**	**33**	**63**

Looking at the right hand total column we see the figures we've already seen in the statement of financial position – the total capital brought forward of 60 and the profit for the year of 3 adding up to 63 in total.

In **limited companies** like this one, **shareholders are paid a return using what are known as dividends.** There were none in this period, and hence the zero. In **privately owned companies payments to the owner or owners as known as drawings.**

Finally, let's examine the share capital and share premium columns. Shares in businesses are issued with a nominal value, often £1 or $1. However that's not necessarily the actual price paid.

In Louie's case, when shareholders put their money into the business they purchased 20,000 x $1 shares, for $30,000. Louis got the full $30,000, but in our records we split that between the **share capital which is based on the nominal value** (20,000 x $1) and the **extra paid on top ($10,000) which is known as the share premium.**

Reserves

You will see items on the statement of financial position and statement of changes in equity called reserves. Let's examine the different types.

Capital reserves

Share capital and share premium: This is the capital paid into the business by the owner or shareholders. In Louie's case, it is $30,000.

Revaluation reserve - this records a change in capital where assets are revalued. If the building was found to be worth more than the $98k carrying value, one option is to revalue this upwards and that increase may be shown in a revaluation reserve.

Revenue reserves (or retained earnings)

Revenue reserves are earnings not paid out to the owners or shareholders. In the example above the $3,000 profit is a revenue reserve. It is often called 'retained earnings'.

Reserves are NOT cash

Profits are put into reserve accounts, but they should not be equated to funds of cash. People often make this mistake. They'll look at Louie's statement of changes in equity and think he's got $63,000 to spend or perhaps just the retained earnings of $33,000. Neither statement is true. In fact we can see from the statement of financial position that Louie has just $15,500 of cash available in his bank account to spend!

CIMA BA3 Study Text

Chapter 5

Recording Transactions

1. Introduction

Just as 'money makes the world go round' in our modern consumer-capitalist society, the concept of double entry bookkeeping keeps the accounting system running!

Although accounting is kept logical by the double-entry process, it can be confusing to implement and understand at times.

So far we know that transactions are initially recorded in the daybooks before they get to the individual ledgers (e.g. sales ledger, purchases ledger, nominal ledger).

We also know that the nominal ledger uses the principle of double-entry bookkeeping. It's therefore vital that accountants learn how to use double-entry in all scenarios.

To tackle this issue, we're going to take a look at how certain kinds of transaction are recorded in the nominal ledger accounts. Specifically, discounts, sales tax and accruals and prepayments, employee pay and bad and doubtful debts.

First, however, let's recap the DEADCLIC process of double entry and think about the different kinds of accounts we use in the bookkeeping process as this is vital to being able to tackle this chapter.

2. Methods of transaction

There are several different ways that transactions can be made.

Cheque

A person making out a cheque is referred to as a drawer. The drawer makes a cheque out to a payee. So, when Business M writes a cheque to the landlord for rent, Business M is the drawer and the landlord is the payee.

The transaction is recorded in to the drawer's (Business M's) ledger right away, whilst the cheque is sent to the payee (the landlord). **Once the payee receives the cheque, they will pay it into their bank using a paying-in slip.**

The payee's bank then makes sure there are sufficient funds in the drawer's account before processing the transaction.

When the funds are transferred between the accounts, the cheque has been cleared. If a cheque does not clear (due to insufficient funds) then it may be returned as dishonoured.

BACS (Banker's Automated Clearing System)

Rather than waiting around for a cheque to be cleared, we can use BACS to make automated payments by providing a list of payments to be made at a specific time. This essentially 'cuts out the middle man' and saves time by having a bank make immediate transfers.

On the downside, this only applies to one-off transactions. So if Business M wanted to make a regular payment of rent to the landlord using BACS, this payment would need to be performed manually each month, which could become bothersome.

Direct Debit or Standing Order

Similar to BACS, although the key difference here is that **a direct debit/standing order can be totally automated**. So if Business M has a regular payment such as rent, the business can arrange to have this paid automatically on a set date every week/month/etc.

Bank-Initiated Transactions

And finally, we have bank-initiated transactions, which are the transaction a bank will make on its own behalf for charges incurred when using their services (such as overdraft fees, processing, account maintenance etc.).

3. Account types

The ledger runs on a system of double-entry. The concept of DEADLIC helps us to decide how to record particular transactions, so that they are in-line with the double-entry process.

We know that if a transactions shows an increase in an asset, it should be debited to that asset account, because we always DEBIT an INCREASE in assets.

For example, if a company makes £100 from sales, and this money goes into the company bank, the company bank account (which is an ASSET account) should be DEBITED with £100.

Generally, assets and liabilities are fairly easy to distinguish from one another. But what about all of the other types of accounts mentioned in DEADCLIC? What are expense accounts, drawings accounts, income accounts and capital or equity accounts?

Let's look at some simple explanations:

Debit an increase in:

- Expense accounts. These are accounts which represent money going out of the business to pay for operations. e.g. rent, salaries.

- Asset accounts. These are accounts which represent things that a company owns, which hold monetary value. e.g. machinery, property.

- Drawings accounts. These are accounts which represent amounts of money being taken from the business by its owners.

Credit an increase in:

- Liabilities accounts. These are accounts which represent money that a company owes. e.g. bank loan, receivables.

- Income accounts. These are accounts which represent the money coming into the business as a result of goods or services sold.

- Capital accounts. These are accounts which represent money invested by or due to owners.

Let's have a look at some examples:

Type of account	Examples
Expense	Bank fees, cost of goods sold, advertising, office supplies, asset losses
Asset	Accounts receivable (due from customers), bank, cash, inventory, land and buildings (often known as PPE – Plant, Property, Equipment)
Drawings	Drawings
Liability	Accounts payable (to suppliers), bank loan, credit card, mortgage

Type of account	Examples
Income	Sales, interest, investment income
Capital	Net Income (Retained Earnings), equity paid into the business

So, if the transaction shows an increase in money coming INTO either an expense account, an assets account or a drawings account, it should be DEBITED to that account.

On the reverse of this, if the transaction shows an increase in money coming INTO a liability account, an income account or a capital account, it should be CREDITED to that account.

4. Discounts

Now, let's look at how we account for discounts.

A discount is a reduction in the price of a product or service. It's likely you're familiar with the concept of discounts; most people will have purchased items from stores or online retailers at a discounted price before.

A business can issue and receive discounts, which fall into the following categories:

Trade discounts

This is a discount which is intended to be used on products sold to people who will then sell them on again (e.g. if you own a corner shop and buy newspapers from a wholesaler).

It is the net value of the product after its discount that is recorded in the ledger.

Example

Let's say John buys a bicycle for his bicycle shop from an online company, OBC. The bicycle has a listed price of £400, subject to a trade discount of 25%. This makes the value of the discount £100, which is subtracted from the listed price, leaving the net value of the bicycle at £300.

John's nominal ledger: In John's ledger, the purchase expenses account is debited with £300.

Purchasing inventory or stock is a cost involved in running John's business. It is therefore an **Expense** which is a **D**ebit using the **DEAD CLIC** rule.

He will now owe this money to OBC though, a **Liability** which is a **Credit** using DEAD CL**I**C.

Dr	Purchase expenses	£300	
Cr	Payables (OBC)		£300

Note how **it is the net value of the product after its discount that is recorded in the ledger**.

OBC's nominal ledger: Meanwhile, in OBC's books, their sales account is **C**redited with the £300 they will receive from John because this is **I**ncome to them (DEAD CL**I**C).

On the other side of the double entry they are owed money from John (a receivable). Increasing an **A**sset is a **D**ebit (De**AD** clic).

Dr	Receivables (John)	£300	
Cr	Sales		£300

Cash discounts

Cash discounts are discounts which apply for a limited time. They are used to encourage trade customers to pay for goods in cash at the time of (or soon after) a sale (rather than the credit this is traditionally offered to trade customers).

The problem with cash discounts is that they are often taken after the original transaction is booked. e.g. Book a purchase of £100 on the purchase date, but then receive the discount a day or two later – another transaction which also needs to be recorded. Let's see how this works.

Example

The Online Bike Company, OBC, sell goods on credit (meaning customers can buy now, pay later). They offer a cash discount of 10% for payments made within 5 days of purchase, on top of their trade discount.

At the time of his purchase, John isn't sure if he can afford to make the payment within the cash discount time frame, and so he records the price of the bike in his purchases and OBC's payable accounts as the list price of £300.

He fills out his accounts using the same method as we saw previously for a credit purchase:

Purchase expense			
01st Jan	Payables (OBC)	300	

Payables (OBC)			
	01st Jan	Purchase exp.	300

However, the next day, John finds that he can afford to make the payment in time to receive the discount, and so pays OBC the discounted sum of **£270**.

Firstly let's record the £270 payment. Paying out of the bank is reducing an asset and so it is a credit to the bank ledger. This will look like this:

Bank			
	02nd Jan	Payables (OBC)	270

On the other side of the transaction John reduces the amount owed to OBC as he's now paid them.

Payables (OBC)			
02nd Jan	Bank	270	01st Jan Purchase exp. 300

However, notice now that we've still got £30 left as owed to OBC. That's obviously wrong as John has taken the discount so does not owe them anything!

A final adjusting entry is required. The £30 discount John has received from OBC is classed as income in his accounts. We credit this increase in income (dead CIIc) into a discounts received account. This account shows the discounts John has received from suppliers.

Discounts received			
	02nd Jan	Payables (OBC)	30

astranti
financial training

The corresponding double entry is a debit entry in the payables account. This reduces the amount the John owes to OBC.

Payables (OBC)					
02nd Jan	Bank	270	01st Jan	Purchase exp.	300
02nd Jan	Discounts received	30			

So the payables account is now zero, as it should be as nothing is owed to OBC by John.

In OBC's books, the discount allowed to John is debited as an expense (DEad clic) in a discounts allowed account, with a corresponding credit entry in the receivables account to reduce the amount John owes to the company.

5.   Sales tax

What is sales tax?

Almost all items that are sold have sales tax attached to them. Therefore, if you have ever purchased an item before, it is very likely that you have paid sales tax.

In the UK this tax is called Value Added Tax (VAT) and is typically included in the price of the item, if it applies to that item. But in other countries, such as the USA, sales tax is not usually included in the price of the item, and is added to the bill when a transaction is made.

Who pays sales tax?

Businesses and individuals pay sales tax when they purchase items. A business will pay sales tax on the items it purchases from suppliers, and will receive sales tax on the goods it sells to customers.

However, **the sales tax that a business receives from customers does not belong to the business** – it is a taxation amount that goes to a taxation authority, and it ultimately paid to the government.

For example, lets say Mr T purchases an item for £500 from Company O. Let's say there's 25% of sales tax included in that payment.

So how much tax was paid? Your initial instinct might be to say well, it's 25% of £500 which is £125. But you'd be wrong!

Tax is paid on the before tax amount. In this case the sales amount was £400, and the tax rate of 25% means that there's £100 (£400 x 25%) of tax.

This can be shown as follows:

Final amount paid after tax   = Sales value before tax x (1 + tax rate)

                                        = £400 x (1 + 0.25)

                                        = £500

Rearranging this formula, **if we are given the final amount we can always work out the original amount as follows:**

$$\text{Sales value before tax} = \frac{\text{Final amount after tax}}{(1 + \text{tax rate})}$$

$$= \frac{£500}{(1 + 0.25)}$$

$$= £400$$

So, for this purchase from Mr T, Company O owes £100 to the tax authorities.

The amount a business 'receives' in sales tax from customers does not affect the revenue of that business, since sales tax goes straight from the business to the taxation authority.

£400 in revenue from this sale to Mr T, and £100 in tax liabilities (the amount is a liability since they owe it to an external party).

Tax reclaimable on purchases

Equally, a business will pay sales tax on goods that it purchases.

If the business is a registered business, the sales tax amount will be able to be reclaimed from the tax authorities. By this we mean **that the amount of sales tax a business has paid to other companies will be deducted from the amount of sales tax they owe to the tax authorities.**

So, lets say when Company O buys stock from their supplier for a total of £400 and there is a 25% sales tax. Let's calculate the original amount:

$$\text{Sales value before tax} = \frac{\text{Final amount after tax}}{(1 + \text{tax rate})}$$

$$= \frac{£400}{(1 + 0.25)}$$

$$= £320$$

£80 was sales tax. That means, this £80 will be able to be claimed back from the tax authorities.

So, remember that when Company O sold Mr T some goods, they received an £100 payment of sales tax from him. They now owe this to the tax authorities.

But, since Company O is also owed £80 from the tax authorities for the purchases it made, we can offset these two amounts against each other:

£100 - £80 = £20

So because of these two transactions, Company O only owe the tax authorities £20.

So, as we have seen, during the course of trading, **a business will both pay and receive sales tax. A business will keep track of all the tax they have paid to suppliers and all the tax they have been paid by customers, and offset these two amounts against each other to get an overall amount of sales tax owed to them, or that they owe to the authorities.**

Output vs input tax

Now another thing to note is that **the tax a company receives from its customers is called 'output tax' and the tax that they pay to their suppliers is called 'input tax'.**

Let's revisit Company O. The £100 that they owe to the tax authorities from their sale of goods to Mr T, is their output tax.

The £80 that they are owed from the tax authorities is their input tax.

Think of it like this: sales tax received from customers is paid on goods going OUT of the company and is therefore output tax, and sales tax paid on purchases is paid on goods coming IN to the company and is therefore input tax.

Accounting for sales tax

When it comes to accounting for sales tax, **the value of goods must be recorded separately from the sales tax**. This is because we use the value and cost of goods to calculate the net profit for a business in a given period, and this should not be effected by the amount of tax paid or received.

Example

Let's return to Company O. Company O sell bicycles in their shop to many different customers. Company O also often purchase bikes from the same online bicycle retailer that we looked at earlier, OBC.

Below is a list of transactions in which Company O have been recently involved (figures are before sales tax):

01ˢᵗ November: Company O purchases £800 worth of helmets from OBC for cash, with a 25% trade discount.

03ʳᵈ November: Company O makes sales on helmets of £60 to Alan Barker (AB) for cash. These originally cost O £30.

Each transaction is subject to the standard sales tax of 20% which is not included in the figures above.

Solution

With regards to the first transaction, we know that Company O made of £600 from OBC. The original price for the items was £800, but Company O received a 25% discount, giving us:

£800 x 0.75 = £600

Company O will have had to pay sales tax on this transaction. We know that sales tax is not included in the amounts shown and is charged at 20%, so:

£600 x 1.20 = £720

Therefore, the total amount Company O paid for the goods was £720 including sales tax. We know that the sales tax and the purchase price have to be recorded separately:

- £600 purchase price

- £120 sales tax

Now, the total amount that has left the bank account as a result of this transaction is £720, so this amount needs to be credited to the bank account, since the bank account is an asset account and a decrease in assets is always credited.

So the bank account will look like this:

		Bank	
	01st Nov	Inventory	600
	01st Nov	Sales tax	120

Now we also have to enter these transactions into the inventory account (to recognise the asset – note increasing an asset is a debit) and the sales tax account.

		Inventory	
01st Nov	Bank	600	

		Sales tax	
01st Nov	Bank	120	

The sales tax account is an asset account (as it's money owed from the tax authorities), and an increase in assets is also always debited (**DeAd** clic).

Now, let's try the same process with the sale of goods to AB. As the table shows us, the amount that AB paid for the goods was £60, and on top of this he paid £12 sales tax, making the total £72:

£60 x 1.2 = £72

Therefore, the whole £72 amount needs to be accounted for.

Because this is a sale made by company O, the money received goes INTO the bank. **Because the bank account is an assets account, an increase is debited (DeAd clic).** Therefore £72 is debited into the bank account:

		Bank	
03rd Nov	Sales	60	
03rd Nov	Sales tax	12	

The sales account is an income account, and an increase in income is always credited (dead **ClIc**):

	Sales	
	03rd Nov Bank	60

The other £12 is recorded in the sales tax account. The sales tax account is an asset account, a decrease in assets is always credited:

		Sales tax		
01st Nov Bank	120	03rd Nov Bank		12

And just like that, the sale of goods to AB is also accounted for.

However we also need to take account of the fact that that sale also means that inventory has been sold so there's a reduction of an asset (credit). The asset cost £30, and this become an increase in an expense (**DE**ad clic)

		Inventory		
01st Nov Bank	600	03rd Nov Expenses		30

	Expenses	
03rd Nov Inventory	30	

Note therefore that the total profit gained on this transaction was £60 (sales) less £30 (expenses) = £30.

Summary – sales tax

As we have seen, once both transactions have been accounted for, the sales tax account looks like this:

		Sales tax		
01st Nov Bank	£120	03rd Nov Bank		£12

From these two transactions there is a debit balance (an asset) of £108. If there were no other transactions this could be reclaimed from the tax authorities.

Non-current assets and expenses

Just like the purchasing of current assets (assets which can be used up in the short term such as money and inventory), **when a company purchases non-current assets (long-term assets such as buildings, machinery and land), they are ordinarily able to reclaim any sales tax paid on these items back from the tax authorities.**

There are some exceptions as to what kinds of sales tax expenditure can be claimed back, however. The specific rules around this vary depending on the country in which the business is trading.

For example, if a business in the UK pays for a company party for customers, the sales tax incurred on paying for the party is not refundable because there is no exemption from sales tax on entertainment expenses in the UK.

Tax returns

A tax return is the document on which a **summary of the tax position over a period of time is shown. This is then submitted to the tax authorities.**

It is usually necessary to list taxes paid and taxes received separately and so a business will usually have separate accounts for input sales tax and output sales tax (and not combine them as we did in the Company O example.)

Non-registered businesses

If a business is particularly small, or the nature of the product or service they provide is of a certain kind, they will not have to charge sales tax to their customers and thus are known as non-registered businesses.

This also means that **they cannot claim back sales tax on their purchases.** In this case, the non-registered company will not have a sales tax account and will instead include the sales tax in the price of the product.

Zero-rated and exempt supplies

The sale of some goods and services are charged at a rate of 0%, and we call these goods zero-rated products (e.g. in the UK, books are one example). **Businesses that supply these goods or services are able to put zero sales tax on their outputs, and can still claim tax refunds on their inputs.**

It is also possible for the sale of certain goods and services to be exempt from sales tax altogether (e.g. In the UK, private healthcare). In some cases, a business that is exempt from sales tax altogether may be at a disadvantage because they are unable to claim a refund on the taxes they pay when making purchases. This will affect the overall profit, since the

sales tax will be added to their cost of sales making it more expensive. This will serve to bring down profit.

6.   Corporation tax

Corporation tax in the financial statements

Corporate entities pay tax on their taxable profits called corporation tax.

Unlike sole traders, for whom tax is a personal expense, companies need to show their tax in the financial statements. This is done via the creation of a taxation expense account and a taxation liability account. Let's explore these in some more detail.

Tax estimates

As with many other payments by a company, **taxation payments do not necessarily relate to the accounting period in which they are made**. At the time of preparing the financial statements, the final taxation liability for the period is not yet known. Confirmation of the final value must await the submission of the corporate tax return and any enquiries made by the tax authorities. This can take a while, particularly if the authorities do not agree!

Due to these necessary time delays, an **estimate of the corporation tax payable** for the period is made at the time of preparation of the financial statements and included within them. This means that the taxation figure in the statements in each year is usually subject to some adjustments.

This means that there are generally two elements to the tax charge in the accounts for any period:

- **Tax payable for the current accounting period** - This will be the tax estimate that we mentioned a moment ago, since tax for the current period will only ever be confirmed by the authorities in a later period.

- **Adjustments to the tax charge for previous accounting periods** - These will be any changes required to the tax charge based on differences between the estimated tax and the final amount that was paid.

Tax accounting

The **corporation tax is debited to a tax expense** account based on the estimated tax payable for the year.

The balance on this account is shown on the statement of financial position (balance sheet) at the accounting year end as a taxation credit or debit, depending on whether we owe tax, or are owed a refund:

For example:

Dr	Taxation expense	£11,150
Cr	Tax liability	£11,150

Here, we have a simple example where we debit a current taxation charge of £11,150 in the profit and loss account and credit a tax liability of the same amount in the statement of financial position (balance sheet). Remember though, this figure is our estimate, and it may change once the tax authorities have reviewed it.

Making adjustments

Okay, so let's say we submit our tax computation for this first year (let's call it Year 1), but it isn't until the following year (Year 2) that the tax authorities get back to us and decide that our final tax liability for Year 1 should have been £12,000. We take a look at their calculations and decide that they are correct and agree on £12,000 as the tax liability for Year 1.

In addition, we have now come to the end of Year 2 and have calculated a new tax liability of £13,500 for the year.

So now what? How to we make the adjustment? Let's summarise:

	Year 1 (£)	Year 2 (£)
Current tax estimate	11,150	13,500
Final tax payable	12,000	-
Tax adjustment required	850	-

For Year 2, we are going to charge current tax of £13,500 as usual, but we are also going to include an adjustment of £850 in respect of Year 1. This means the taxation liability for Year 2 is £13,500 + £850 = £14,350.

CIMA BA3 Study Text

Chapter 6

The Regulatory Framework

1. Assumptions of accounting

The practice of accounting is based on some **basic underlying assumptions**. These assumptions are the **principles upon which financial statements are produced**.

As we will see in the next section, these **assumptions form the basis of conceptual frameworks** (which more specific, formalised accounting rules stem from). For now, just bare in mind that these assumptions of accounting, as shown below, underpin **the way all accounting is carried out**.

Materiality

This is the convention of only including relevant information in the financial statements. Small, insignificant transactions that won't affect the view obtained by the reader of the accounts are less important. A small error of £100 in the accounts of a billion pound company can be ignored as it makes little difference to the reader. A £100m error must be corrected however as by not doing so the reader will be mislead as to the actual financial position of the business.

Let's look at another example. J Shoes Ltd, is a manufacturer and retailer of shoes who have to purchase storage boxes for shoe-making equipment. The boxes are a minimal cost, but are also technically assets that will be used over a long period of time. Rather than using the more complicated accounting approach for assets, they can simply be recorded as an expense, since this cost will not significantly affect the calculation of the profit.

The general rule here is that items that together make up less than 5% of the net profit (the actual profit after all expenses are paid) **is considered as immaterial.**

Going concern

The going concern principle assumes that **a business will continue its business activities for the foreseeable future.**

If this is not the case and the company is already looking at the possibility of a reduction in the scale of its business activities or ending business activities altogether, **the financial statements must be drawn up on a different basis,** taking this into account. This situation would need to be **disclosed in the accounts,** to avoid **misleading** the users.

Accruals basis

The idea behind the accruals basis assumption is that **transaction will be matched to the period in which they occur.** Therefore, transactions and events are reported in the financial statements for the accounting period in which the actual transactions take place, and **not for the period when the cash is paid or received.**

For example, J Shoes Ltd make a sale on 31ˢᵗ December (the company's year end), but the cash is not received until sometime in the following year. Under an accruals basis, the sale should be **recorded as relating to the year of the sale, not the year in which the cash was received.**

The **related costs** also have to be shown in that year too, ensuring that **everything related to that transaction is matched to the same accounting period** and ensuring a fair representation is given in the accounts.

Substance over form

The principle of substance over form dictates that **transactions are reflected in the accounts so that the users are seeing the economic reality,** even if that means the *legal form* is over-ridden.

For example, let's say J Shoes Ltd's warehouse is actually owned by another company, but is legally leased for it's whole life to J Shoes Ltd.

Although J Shoes Ltd do not **technically own the asset, in reality they are getting the full use of the asset for its life,** and the 'substance' or **reality** is that **they own the asset in every practical sense,** and so the warehouse should be treated as if they own it in their financial records.

Business entity convention

This is the principle of separating individuals involved in the business from the business itself. Sole traders and partnerships are thought of as using their business as a vehicle to make profit. **A limited company is seen as a separate entity completely compared with its shareholders and staff and the limited company's accounts are prepared independently of any transactions those individuals enter into personally.**

Prudence

Prudence simply means **being realistic and not overly optimistic.** This could apply, for example, when calculating figures such as the valuation of stock, where **a realistic (or even slightly pessimistic view)** of the value of the stock should be chosen.

Another example would be the view taken about the business's ability to recover its debts. As soon as it looks unlikely that the debt will be paid back then that should be shown in the accounts.

Why would this be useful in accounting? Well, the thought is that one should be **as realistic as possible,** and when it comes to a call of judgement, pessimism is best. This is **because if the worst should happen, investors will be prepared, and if something good should happen, then it's a bonus!**

Consistency convention

This convention ensures that we **treat items consistently between periods**.

An example of this is making sure we use the same methods of calculating the costs associated with long-term assets (depreciation) each and every year. If the policy changed each year it would become very confusing for readers and that's something which accountants try to avoid (although they may not always succeed!)

Fair presentation

The **financial statements should be a "fair" presentation of the financial position, performance, and cash flows, so that those reading them understand the full effect of transactions that have taken place.**

For example, a manager asks the accountant to treat a new machine purchased as an expense rather than an asset as it will save the company tax in the short term. Doing so would not be a fair presentation of the nature of the asset and would be wrong.

Fair presentation will usually have been achieved if the business follows all International Financial Reporting Standards (which we will look at soon) when preparing the financial statements. The business must must also make a statement in the accounts to confirm this has been the case.

Historic cost convention

This measure means that the price of an asset in a financial report is shown at its original cost (otherwise known as the nominal cost).

For example, if J Shoes Ltd purchase a machine for £100,000, they would continue to record its original cost as £100,000 even if its resale value increases to £110,000 or decreases to £90,000. The cost includes any costs in bringing the asset to its current location and condition. If J Shoes were charged £1,000 for delivery and installation of the machine, the historic cost would be £101,000.

Money measurement convention

In terms of accounting the assumption is that **an item can be included in the financial statements if and only if that item can be reliably measured in monetary terms.**

This is a fair assumption most of the time – after all business transactions are almost always in monetary terms e.g. a purchase or a sale. However it's not always the case: for example, if an entity owns a brand, but is unable to get a reliable estimate of its value in terms of any known currency. In this situation the item, the brand in the case, should not be included in the financial statements.

Stable monetary unit convention

Imagine for a moment a business in Country B, with B$1m of revenues in one year and B$2m of revenues in the next.

That sounds like the business has done exceedingly well during the period, until we learn that that Country B has very high inflation of 100% and they actually simply sold the same number of units for double the price – just like most other companies in that country.

When examining financial statements from one year to the next, the high inflation is not apparent as all that is seen is the monetary figures of S$1m and S$2m. That's unfair on the reader of the accounts who might get the wrong idea of the business performance.

The stable monetary unit convention says that we should assume that **monetary units are stable and dependable such that inflation is so low that when producing accounts and comparing them year by year that inflation can be ignored.**

Now while that wouldn't be the case in Country B, in most countries in the real world, the effect of inflation is small and the comparisons are fair. In countries like Country B, where it might not be fair then this assumption might not be able to be applied and inflation adjustments made.

Dual aspect convention

This convention underlies the practice of double entry bookkeeping. The basic idea is that **every transaction has two aspects that should be recorded in the entity's accounts.**

For example, when a company purchases inventory to be sold on to customers at a later date, the transaction would involve a payment of funds (a decrease in the bank account) and the receipt of inventory (an increase in the inventory account). Thus, each transaction must be shown as two aspects in the entity.

Assumptions In Accounting	**Materiality** - only relevant information goes in the statements
	Going concern - the business will continue its activities for the foreseeable future
	Accrual basis - transactions are matched to the period they occurred in
	Substance over form - transaction show economic reality rather than simply legal form
	Business entity convention - individuals involved in a business are kept separate from the business itself
	Prudence - accountants have a realistic outlook when preparing statements
	Consistency convention - treat items consistently between periods
	Fair presentation- economic position of a the business is accurately reflected in the statements
	Historic cost convention - the price of an asset is shown at its original cost
	Stable monetary unit convention - assumes low inflation between periods
	Money measurement convention – items only included if they can be measured reliably in monetary terms
	Dual aspect convention - all transactions have two aspects (a debt and a credit)

2. The regulatory framework

The phrase 'financial reporting' refers to the process of using financial statements to convey information about a business to investors.

In order to maintain consistency across the financial statements of companies, financial reporting is strictly regulated. This is achieved by developing accounting standards.

Unfortunately, **there aren't yet any universal accounting standards,** and there are some **differences in accounting depending on where in the world you go.**

What we will take a look at in this section is how these differences impact the implementation of accounting standards as well as the regulation of the profession more generally.

Conceptual frameworks

The **conceptual framework for accounting details broad principles to be used in accounting.** From there the process of developing accounting standards (which are the more specific rules) occurs against the backdrop of this well-known conceptual framework.

To demonstrate what I mean, let's consider the common rules we see at a swimming pool: no running, no diving in the shallow end, no shouting, etc.

The guiding principle that the swimming pool owner has in mind when drawing up these specific rules is to keep people safe. This is their framework for the pool rules, in the same way conceptual frameworks for accountancy are the frameworks for accounting standards (which are also specific rules).

The conceptual framework deals with fundamental financial reporting issues such as:

- the objectives and users of financial statements,

- the characteristics that make accounting information useful,

- the basic elements of financial statements (e.g. assets, liabilities, equity, income, and expenses),

- how transactions are recognised and measured in the financial statements.

More specific rules for these areas are then **created with these conceptual frameworks in mind.**

Local regulatory frameworks

These are frameworks which operate within counties, that **govern how companies within those countries should practice accounting**. Local regulatory frameworks are **governed by 3 main factors:**

- **The accounting requirements of the national law.** For example, a UK company will be required to abide by the relevant legislation in the UK, such as the Companies Act.

- **The accounting standards applying in the local jurisdiction**, as set by and monitored by the local accounting regulators. For example, a company from the UK will have to follow all the standards that make up the Generally Accepted Accounting Practice (or GAAP) in the UK.

- **Accounting requirements as laid out by the country's stock exchange** as required for companies that want to be listed on that stock exchange. For example, all listed companies in the UK must follow the International Financial Reporting Standards (IFRSs) set out by the International Accounting Standards Board (IASB). You'll become more familiar with these groups later on.

International regulation

In addition to local regulation there is an international dimension of regulation, consisting of:

- The requirements of **relevant international accounting bodies**

- **International financial reporting standards (IFRSs)**

- **A conceptual framework developed at an international level**

The extent of use of international accounting standards varies from country to country. In some countries, international accounting standards have been adopted as the local standards. In others a choice can be offered, and often larger companies may elect to use international accounting standards.

For example, in the UK the local framework is set by the Financial Reporting Council (FRC), but businesses also have to abide by the international standards set by the International Financial Reporting Standards (IFRS) Foundation.

Certain countries also have to take account of international organisations and their regulatory requirements. The European Union (EU) for example, issues Directives that must be implemented by its member states.

Requirements in respect of companies listed on a stock exchange are influenced by a body called the International Organisation of Securities Commissions (IOSCO).

The influence of international accounting standards is increasing, and this is due to the convenience of having one standard for all, making international trade much less cumbersome. Most standards across the globe are becoming more and more in line with international standards, and this can mean significant changes in the current practice of those countries when they make the change.

Gradual approach to international convergence

Adopting the international accounting standards generally involves a process of transition and adaptation for companies and governments.

Although the policy of adopting international accounting standards ensures consistency with other countries, it may lead to problems owing to a disparity between the requirements of the international standards and the traditions and level of development of the country using them.

Some countries are moving gradually to align their national standards with international accounting standards. **A gradual approach to convergence rather than changing everything at once is often preferable as it makes the change process easier.** This

alignment needs to be gradual enough for businesses and stakeholders to have time to adjust to the transition.

Generally Accepted Accounting Practise (GAAP)

In any given country there is a generally agreed approach to accounting.

This agreed approach is referred to as the **Generally Accepted Accounting Practice (GAAP)**. This term is employed to describe **the accounting rules, procedures and practices used in a country.**

The GAAP includes regulations applicable in its particular jurisdiction, and will therefore be different in different countries. Because of changes to rules and regulations, the GAAP will also change over time within the same jurisdiction.

3. International Accounting Standards Board (IASB)

As we have seen, there are international accounting standards which are increasingly being adopted worldwide to ensure consistency and comparability in the financial statements. But **who is responsible for setting these standards and making sure they are implemented and followed appropriately?**

In this section we'll take a look at the key bodies involved in this process, and tell you a little about how it works. It's a bit dull I know, but you've got to learn this for the exam!

IFRS Foundation

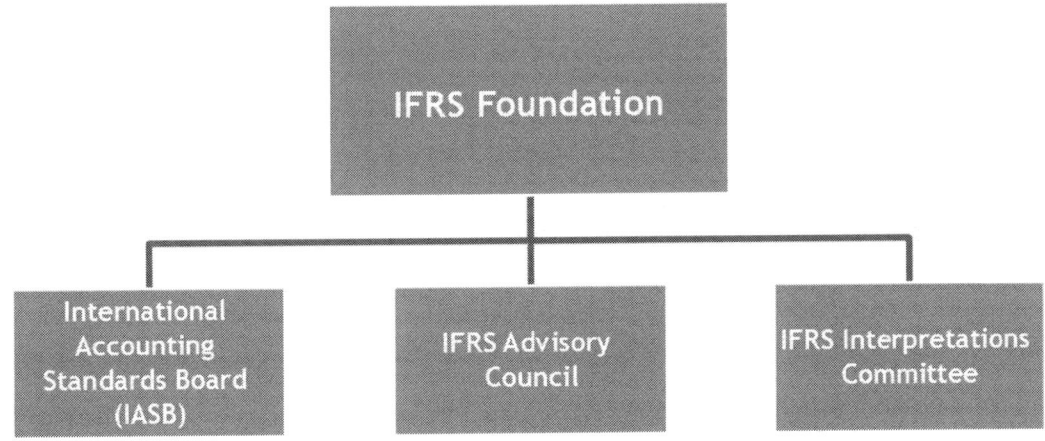

IFRS Foundation

Think of the IFRS Foundation as a board of directors at the very top of a company. They are the ones in charge of all of the other bodies.

IFRS stands for International Financial Reporting Standards. International Financial Reporting Standards are global accounting standards (international rules for accountancy), and the IFRS Foundation has the ultimate responsibility for **developing theses standards.**

Financial reporting standards are developed with the intention of making sure that all financial statements are clear, understandable and easy to compare to those of other companies.

The IFRS Foundation's core objectives are:

- To develop, in the public interest (this means for the benefit of everyone), **a single set of high quality, understandable, enforceable and globally-accepted financial reporting standards** based upon clear principles.

- To **promote** the use and **rigorous application** of those standards.

- In fulfilling the above objectives, **to take account of a diverse range economic settings.** This basically means that the standards should accommodate for the fact that businesses can be all different sizes and be functioning in all different markets under all different sorts of conditions. Therefore, the standards shouldn't be restricting for any kind of businesses.

- **To promote and facilitate adoption of International Financial Reporting Standards (IFRSs),** through the convergence (adapting) of national accounting standards and IFRSs. Basically, to encourage and help the standards to be used internationally!

Trustees

The **IFRS Foundation consists of 22 Trustees** who are responsible for appointing the members of the other subsidiary bodies – the IASB, the IFRS Advisory Council and the IFRS Interpretations Committee.

To ensure that the **Trustees are representative of different regions of the world,** there are always a certain number of Trustees from North America, Europe and the Asia/Oceania region and from elsewhere in the world.

The Trustees represent various interested groups such as leading accounting firms, preparers and users of accounts, the academic world and other interested parties. They are **not involved in the technical matters relating to accounting standards themselves.**

Funding

Funding for the IFRS Foundation is provided by several bodies; the International Federation of Accountants (IFAC), which is the global organisation for the accountancy profession; **professional accountancy organisations** internationally such as **ICAEW, CIMA and ACCA, and** from **financial institutions and accounting firms.**

Its members include more than 150 accounting organisations from more than a hundred countries worldwide.

International Accounting Standards Board (IASB)

The IASB are responsible for **actually developing and managing the international accounting standards.** Think of the IASB as the production department who are in charge of producing the main product of the 'company' – the accounting standards. Their specific roles include:

- Issuing **'exposure drafts'** (drafts of proposed new standards release for public comment).

- **Preparing** and **publishing** the international financial reporting standards (IFRS) themselves.

- **Approving the interpretations** that are prepared by the IFRS Interpretations Committee (see below).

The IASB liaises directly with the national bodies responsible for setting local accounting standards to promote the convergence of national accounting standards.

IFRS and IAS

International Financial Reporting Standards (**IFRS**) are the **accounting standards** prepared under the **current system of international regulation.**

International Accounting Standards (IAS) are the accounting standards prepared under the previous system of international regulation. The IASs, as the old standards, have all been adopted by the IASB. The old and new standards therefore have **the same status.**

IFRS Interpretations Committee

Once standards have been set, **different companies may interpret the standards differently.** As a result of these different interpretations, the accounting treatment of some transactions could differ widely between companies and some of these accounting methods might not be acceptable.

The **IFRS Interpretations Committee** therefore looks at these complex situations within the context of particular financial reporting standards and **issues guidance**. This helps to **promote** a more **uniform practical application of the standard**.

For example, the IFRS Interpretations Committee proposed an amendment to a standard known as IAS 12 – Income Taxes, based on how to interpret "the accounting for deferred tax assets for unrealised losses on debt instruments measured at fair value."

The meaning of this particular amendment does not need to be understood by you right now, this is just an example to demonstrate that what the IFRS Interpretations Committee do is highly technical. It is their job is to make sure that guidelines **leave no room for ambiguity or error, so that the standards can be applied consistently and correctly in any situation.**

The **procedure** adopted by the IFRS Interpretations Committee is to:

- Issue a **draft interpretation of one of the standards for public comment.**

- After consideration of the interpretation the **twelve voting members** take a decision on **finalising the interpretation**. If only three or fewer of the voting members oppose the interpretation of the standard, it goes forward to the IASB.

- Once gaining **IASB approval** they **publish the interpretation**, and from this point on accountants **who prepare accounts** under the IFRS **must comply** with the provisions of the interpretation.

So, try to think of the Interpretations Committee as **quality control**, checking that rules as set out by the standards are being applied correctly and if not, **proposing edits to the standards to makes sure they can be applied uniformly, without ambiguity**. This ensures that all IFRS financial statements are all reliable, consistent and comparable.

IFRS Advisory Council

So, finally we come to the link between the IASB and the **views of the wider public.**

Through the **IFRS Advisory Council,** the wider view on the ongoing projects for new and revised accounting standards can be communicated to the IASB.

The organisation can also give other types of advice including the **projects that should be on the agenda** of the IASB and the **most pressing priorities to be addressed** in the IASB's future work program.

The IFRS Advisory Council has at least **30 members** appointed for terms of three years which can then be renewed.

So, think of the advisory council as similar to the customer service team in an organisation who are in touch with the wider public. They take into consideration the views of their customers, and present the findings to the IASB.

4. Qualitative characteristics of financial information

In order to have good statements across the board, we need something to make sure that the information contained within the statements meets certain standards to ensure the information presented is of a high quality.

The IASB provides the following list of **6 qualitative characteristics of financial information**:

- **Understandability**

- **Relevance**

- **Faithful representation**

- **Comparability**

- **Verifiability**

- **Timeliness.**

Let's have a look at each in more detail.

Understandability

In at number one: Understandability. Obviously, the accounting information provided must be **easy for the user to interpret**. However, the users are assumed to have reasonable business and accounting knowledge and to be prepared to study the financial information carefully.

Therefore, the preparer of financial statements should not shy away from including complex information if it is necessary to understand the financial position of the company. The preparer should **not exclude relevant information from the accounts on the grounds that users will have difficulty in understanding it.**

Relevance

Number two on our list is relevance. This means that the information in the financial statements **must be relevant to the users**. It is considered to be relevant if it **helps the users to make investment decisions or other economic decisions.**

Investors will want to know information such as revenues, expenses, assets, liabilities, cash flows and profits. They won't want to know what's on the menu at the company canteen, that a junior member of staff left during the year, or what happened at the Christmas party!

The financial statements should also guide users to make reasoned judgements about economic events that the business has been involved in, and to a fair judgement on the current and likely future financial position of a business.

The **information also needs to be complete** so that rational decisions can be based on it. If the financial statements only included half the transactions for the year it would not be useful.

Faithful representation

'Faithful representation' is another way of saying **reliable**. The statements need to **paint an accurate picture of the business.**

On top of that, the information **should not contain any errors** or any **biased assumptions**. It should therefore be presented in a neutral and impartial way.

Comparability

The decision to invest in the shares of one company rather than another requires the **ability to compare the financial performance of one company to another**. The financial statements must therefore enable the user to make **comparisons between entities** and also to make **comparisons over time of the performance of the same entity**.

When a user compares the financial statements of two entities the accounting policies used must be clear, so that any difference between the accounting policies of the two entities are apparent to the user and appropriate conclusions can be drawn.

The disclosure of accounting policies is therefore an important feature of financial statements. It is also essential to include comparative figures from the prior period.

Verifiability

Verifiability helps to assure users that the provided information actually shows what it claims to show. **Does the information provided lend itself to verification by an external source**, such as an audit? Yes? Well, then it is verifiable.

Financial information is generally **supported by real evidence** (such as receipts and purchase orders) and independent individuals can check one against the other to see whether the information is faithfully represented.

Timeliness

In at number six we have timeliness. Timeliness means **providing information to decision-makers in time to be capable of influencing their decisions**. It shouldn't be significantly delayed or else it will be of little or no value.

Example

Let's take a section of some financial statements and see which of the qualities it has, and which it doesn't. Let's take the line for their net profit, from the company's income statement:

	20X5	20X4
	£m	£m
Net profit	(11)	(9)

Elsewhere in the accounts it states that:

"All financial statements are produced using International Financial Reporting Standards, and an independent audit has verified them. Accounting policies have not changed between 20X4 and 20X5."

Now, let's rate this against the 6 qualities:

Understandability	Almost anyone who uses financial statements will know what net profit is and how it is calculated. **OK.**
Relevance	This is very relevant, since potential investors will look at this figure to see how profitable the company it. If it is low, then investors will look elsewhere. In this company investors may be worried about losses being made two years in a row (that's what the brackets mean in the figures – a negative number). **OK.**
Faithful representation	The fact that an audit has taken place which verifies the numbers, and that they have been prepared using IFRSs would suggest they are a faithful representation of the position of the business. **OK.**
Comparability	Producing the profit figure using IFRSs ensures the figure is comparable with other companies that use those same standards. **OK.** The fact that accounting policies have not changed between the years should mean that the results are comparable between 20X4 and 20X5. **OK.**
Verifiability	The fact an audit has taken place shows the figures were verifiable. **OK.**
Timeliness	There is not enough information available to confirm this – we would need to know when the accounts were published to decide. **Not clear.**

5. Governance and financial reporting

Management will also play a role when it comes to accounting regulation. For a sole trader or partnership business, it will be largely up to the owners how much they do in the way of regulating their accounting.

However, limited companies are slightly different, in that the management work for the company rather than own it, and the owners of the company are the ones who provide the capital for the company.

Since management are required to manage on behalf of the shareholders and owners, they are involved in what is called the stewardship function. This is basically the term given to the manager's role of 'taking care' of the company on behalf of the shareholders.

Managers and directors are ultimately responsible for making sure that their company, and in particular their accounting department, is **producing financial statements according to the appropriate standards.**

CIMA BA3 Study Text

Chapter 7

Accruals, Pay and Bad Debts

1. Accruals and prepayments

Accrued expenses

You probably use electricity, and more than likely the electricity you use today, you will pay for at a later date, sometime after you've been billed. **Accountants typically account for items when used and not when billed** and so if you were doing your own personal accounts for a calendar year – at the end of the year you would need to work out and account for how much electricity you had used which you had yet to be billed for. That's an accrued expense.

Accrued expenses are expenses which are brought into the financial statement for **goods and services that have been received from a supplier, but are yet to be paid for by the business who purchased them.**

Accruals are liabilities, because they are money owed by a business to an external body.

Prepayments

Prepayments are the opposite of accruals, in that they are the **payments for goods or services that have yet to be received.** Prepayments include such things as rent paid in advance.

As the opposite of accruals, prepayments are assets. They are amounts you have paid which you have not yet 'cashed in on' by receiving the corresponding services.

Accounting for accruals and prepayments

When accounting for accruals, a business will usually make an estimate of the charges they expect to pay for the period.

This is done by reference to previous costs for the same period, or by measurements with a meter (such as an electricity meter).

So, for example, if a business has used water, gas or electricity during a certain period but has not yet been charged for it, the business will make an estimate of the electricity based on the typical usage, perhaps with reference to previous bills.

Accounting for prepayments is usually done by breaking up the payment over a time period. It is assumed that a prepayment is incurred evenly over a time period.

So, let's say that the car insurance on Company O's company car is £12,000 for the year. They have to pay the bill at the start of the year, but every month they will charge themselves £1,000 to their expenses account, because:

£12,000 ÷ 12 = £1,000

Therefore, to spread the cost of the insurance over the year in which it is used, £1,000 needs to be expensed every month.

If the company's financial year end came halfway through the year then there will remain an asset of £6,000 which has been paid but not yet used – that's a prepayment.

Matching

Matching is the concept of accounting for expenses within the period in which they were incurred, regardless of when the actual payment is due.

If a product is made today and costs £10 to make. Tomorrow is the end of the accounting year (20X5) and the item is sold on the first day of the following year for £15 (20X6). The costs of that sale should be carried forward to 20X6 so the £10 cost is recorded in the same period as the £15 sale. The sale and it's related expenses are 'matched' in the same time period.

The same argument is used for accruals and prepayments. In the case of our example of rent on a building paid in advance with 6 months outstanding at the year end. The advance payment relates to work which will be done in that building in the following year and so that cost should be matched against income in the following year not in the year it was paid.

Assets or liabilities

When it comes to the statement of financial position, **prepayments are recorded as current assets (short term assets), while accruals are recorded as current liabilities (short term liabilities).**

Recording accruals and prepayments

Example

The following table shows the transactions related to electricity as they relate to the year 20X1:

	£
Accruals b/f	400
Bills received and paid in 20X1	
31st Jan	525
30th April	315
31st July	410
31st Oct	360
Bill received on 31st Jan 20X2	720
	(01st Nov – 31st Jan)

The company needs to record its expenses for the year, which ended on 31st December 20X1.

Let's start with the beginning of the year. There are two accounts:

1) An accruals account, where the liability is recorded.

2) An expenses account for electricity.

Our accruals account starts with a liability showing of £400. This represents electricity charge in the previous year which has yet to have been billed.

Accruals			
20X1	£	20X1	£
		01st Jan Balance b/f	400

The first step is to charge this back to the electricity expense account (Dr Accruals, Cr Electricity). We'll also record the first electricity bill too (it's a debit because it's an expense - **DE**ad clic).

Accruals

20X1		£	20X1		£
			01ˢᵗ Jan	Balance b/f	400
01ˢᵗ Jan	Electricity	400			

Electricity

20X1		£	20X1		£
31ˢᵗ Jan	Bank	525	01ˢᵗ Jan	Accruals	400

At this point notice that the amount charged so far is the £525 bill, less the proportion that relates to the previous year (£400), leaving a total of £125 charged for the year. That relates to January's electricity bill.

Next we'll add in all the other bills for the year:

Electricity

20X1		£	20X1		£
31ˢᵗ Jan	Bank	525	01ˢᵗ Jan	Accruals	400
30ᵗʰ Apr	Bank	315			
31ˢᵗ July	Bank	410			
31ˢᵗ Oct	Bank	360			

We've now got all the months through to October charged for. But what about November and December?

The bill received on 31ˢᵗ Jan 20X2 is £720. Two months of three months relates to 20X1 and so let's work out how much that should be: 2/3 x £720 = £480.

£480 is the year end accrual. It's the amount of **electricity used in the year which has yet to be billed at the year end.**

astranti
financial training

This is then expensed too (a debit), with the other entry going back into the accruals account as there's now a liability at the year end as the company owe the electricity company for the electricity used. We can also balance off the accounts.

Electricity						
20X1		£	20X1			£
31st Jan	Bank	525	01st Jan	Accruals		400
30th Apr	Bank	315				
31st July	Bank	410				
31st Oct	Bank	360				
31st Dec	Accrual	480	31st Dec	Income statement		1690
		2090				2090

As we see, in total £1,690 was the expense for the year. This was transferred to the final income statement for the year where the companies final profit or loss will be shown.

Accruals					
20X1		£	20X1		£
			01st Jan	Balance b/d	400
01st Jan	Electricity	400			
			31st Dec	Electricity	480
31st Dec	Balance b/d	480			
		880			880
			1st Jan	Balance c/d	480

There was also liability of £480 at the end of the year in the accruals account relating to November and December's electricity used but not yet paid. That will be shown in the company's statement of financial position at the year end.

Accrued and prepaid income

Sometimes, accruals and prepayments relate to income as well as expenditure.

Accrued income

Accrued income is **money that has be earned by an entity, but not yet received.**

For example, consider a company that has invested £10,000 on 1st January in a bond with a payment of 4% per annum. The bond pays £200 of interest two times a year: on 1st July and 1st January.

On 31st January, a month has passed since investing in the bond, and so the company will have earned one month's interest. This is calculated as:

£10,000 bond x 4% interest per year x 1/12 of a year = £33.33.

However, no interest will be received by the company in January, since it will be paid as part of the £200 to be received on 1st July. Therefore, the £33.33 of interest earned during January, but not yet received or recorded as of 31st January, is known as accrued income.

At the end of the year, accrued income will have been recorded in the accounts as follows:

Cash was received on 1st July.

Bank

Other income (Interest)	£200		

Other income (Interest)

		Bank	£200

By the end of the year, another £200 of interest is earned, but has yet to be received. As such there is an asset in the Statement of Financial Position of £200 at the year end:

Accrued income (SOFP)

Other income (interest)	£200		

The other side of the double entry is in other income:

Other income (interest)

		Bank	£200
		Accrued income	£200

As always, at the end of the year an income account is closed off and the balance taken to the P&L account so that this can be recognised in the income statement for the year:

Other income (interest)

		Bank	£200
		Accrued income	£200
P&L (income ac.)	£400		
	£400		£400

Prepaid income

Prepaid income functions in the opposite way to accrued income. **It represents income received but not yet earned.**

For example, an entity that has a rental property where the tenant pays in advance. The entity would receive income before it had been earned by letting out the property.

In this case, the accounting is reversed. The income account is debited and **a liability is created for the prepaid income in the statement of financial position.**

Let's try a quick example.

Entity F rents property to tenant T for £600 per month. The tenant pays in advance on the last day of each month (so a payment on 31st January is for the month of February). The tenant moved in on 30th November and the entity's year end is 31st March.

At the reporting date, the entity has earned rent for 4 months (December – March) but has received rent for 5 months (December – April).

As the cash comes in it is booked to the accounts, so at the year end we will have received £3,000:

Bank			
Rent	£3,000		

And booked that to rental income:

Rental Income			
		Bank	£3,000

However, the £3,000 is too high, as the last of the £600 payments was payment in advance for the following year. We must take that out of rental income therefore, and record it as a liability (prepaid income) at the year end.

Rental Income			
Prepaid income	£600	Bank	£3,000
P&L (income st.)	£2,400		
	£3,000		£3,000

When balanced off we see the correct amount for the year of £2,400 is taken to the income statement.

Prepaid income (SOFP)	
Rent	£600

The £600 paid in advance is a current liability as it is money owed to the tenant at the year end in the SOFP.

2. Employee pay

All companies that employ people to work for them will need to pay wages or salaries. Not only do the correct amounts need to be calculated for each employer, but each amount will also be subject to various taxes depending on the country in which the business operates.

In the UK for example, workers pay income tax on their earnings, as well as national insurance (which goes towards healthcare and state pension amongst other things). Workers may also opt in to other voluntary expenses, such as a company gym membership or a private pension.

Example

Wendy works 36.5 hours a week as a personal trainer at a gym. She earns £7.81 an hour, and as she lives in the UK, she pays an income tax of 20% on all her earnings that exceed £192.31 per week. She also pays a national insurance tax of 12% on all her earnings between £153 and £805 per week.

Wendy pays £30 a month for membership at the gym in which she works. Finally, Wendy pays into a company pension scheme, which is 5% of her weekly wages.

Wendy makes 36.5 x £7.81 = £285.07 per week.

Let's figure out how much of that she takes home after taxes:

	£	£
Gross earnings		285.07
Less: income tax ((285.07 – 192.31) x 0.2)	18.55	
N.I. ((285.07 – 153) x 0.12)	15.85	
		(34.40)
Net earnings		250.67
Less: gym membership	6.92	
Pension scheme (285.07 x 0.05)	14.25	
		(21.17)
Net pay to be received		**229.50**

astranti
financial training

So, when Wendy's net pay is calculated, the business knows how much to pay her. Of course, all of this information needs to be recorded in her employer's ledger accounts, and we do that as follows:

Start by recording the total wages in an expense account – hopefully you're getting the idea by now that an expense is a debit (**DE**ad clic)

Wages

Wages payable	285.07		

The other side of the double entry goes into a wages payable account. This records the total due to the member of staff.

Wages payable

	Gross wages	285.07

Of course, of the £285.07, we know that not all of that is paid to Wendy. Some is payable to the tax authorities, the gym and the pension fund. Let's record those amounts. They're debits as they are reducing the amount liability due to Wendy.

Wages payable

N.I. + income tax payable	34.40	Gross wages	285.07
Gym membership payable	6.92		
Pension scheme payable	14.25		

We now have three new T accounts for the amounts owed to these groups though. All are liabilities which is a credit (dead **CL**ic).

Tax payable (N.I. and income tax)

	Wages	34.40

Payables (Gym)

	Wages	6.92

Payables (Pension scheme)

	Wages	14.25

Finally we can balance off the wages payable account to get:

Wages payable			
N.I. + income tax payable	34.40	Gross wages	285.07
Gym membership payable	6.92		
Pension scheme payable	14.25		
Balance c/d	229.50		
	285.07		285.07
		Balance b/d	229.50

Here, the balance brought down is what Wendy will actually receive in her pay cheque! Once that is paid the payable account will go down to zero.

3.   Bad debts and allowances

It's not any fun having to save up for a long time to buy the things we want, and sometimes it's just impractical.

For instance, say Mr T has just spent all of his savings learning to drive, and now he needs to buy a car to get a job. Without the car he can't get the job, but without the job he can't buy a car.

Many businesses will offer credit or payment plans, to encourage people to buy their products even if they don't have the money to pay right away.

Let's say Mr T gets a payment plan so he can get a car straight away and pay for it in little chunks every month. Brilliant, problem solved, both him and the car dealer are very happy. Mr T gets a car he wouldn't have otherwise been able to buy, and the car dealership secures a customer they may have missed out on otherwise.

However, it's not always a happy story. Sometimes someone who has bought something on credit or using a payment scheme fails to make their payments.

Now, apart from this being bad news for a business in terms of profits, it's also annoying for their accountant.

When businesses sell on credit, there is always uncertainty about the ability of customers to pay their debts off. Because of this a business may reasonably allow for a percentage of their receivables to never be paid off.

This makes it much easier to account for failed payments or bad debts as the difference has already been accounted for. This next section will cover this concept in more depth.

Accounting for bad debts

If a business discovers that a customer is unable to pay the full amount that they owe, the business will need to remove the value of the transaction from the receivables account and transfer it to a different kind of account - a bad debt account.

Let's use an example to see how this works.

Example

On 01st January, OBC sells **£200** worth of goods to Chris Parker on credit.

On 05th April, Chris pays **£50** towards the cost of the goods. On 28th November, OBC is told that Chris has been declared bankrupt and is unlikely to be able to pay the remaining debt. This remaining debt has become a bad debt.

Let's see how we manage the accounts to record this bad debt. Let's firstly record the sale and the receipt in the receivables account.

Receivables					
01st Jan	Sales	200	05th Apr	Bank	50

There would be corresponding entries in the sales and bank T accounts but we won't show them at the moment.

On the 28th November a bad debt is recorded. A credit to the receivables account of £150 will completely remove the receivable from the account.

Receivables					
01st Jan	Sales	200	05th Apr	Bank	50
			28th Nov	Bad debts	150
		200			200

Bad debts			
28th Nov	CP	150	

At the end of the accounting year, the balance is transferred to the income statement to record it as an expense in the year end accounts.

Bad debts					
28th Nov	CP	150	31st Dec	Income statement	150

Example – repayment of bad debt

Chris receives some money from a long lost relative and can now pay off his debts. He pays off his remaining debt in January of the next year. OBC's accountant would have to make the following changes in the account.

The first step is to reinstate the amount due into the receivables account (debit as it's an asset). The other side of the double entry does into the bad debt account.

Receivables			
10th Jan	Bad debts	150	

Bad debts			
		10th Jan Receivables	150

Next the amount paid is shown, to pay off the receivable:

Receivables			
10th Jan	Bad debts	150	10th Jan Bank 150

The £150 in the bad debts account would be netted off any other bad debts in the year, and so the extra expense charged in the previous year will end up being netted against bad debts in this year's accounts.

Doubtful debts - Allowance for receivables

In some cases a business will know for sure that a customer will be unable to pay a debt, and this is when it is recorded as a bad debt. However, there are sometimes cases in which a business is only doubtful that a debt will be paid.

Let's say a car company, Speed Ltd, has sold a brand new car on a payment scheme. They should be able to record a revenue of £20,000. However, after paying back just £5,000 of the £20,000, the buyer defaults on several payments in a row. Perhaps they will get their money – but perhaps they will not!

Businesses can estimate the chance of doubtful debts in two different ways:

- **Specific allowances** are calculated for a particular individual of whom a doubtful debts are expected. If it seemed unlikely that the money would be paid in the above case a £15,000 specific allowance could be made against this car.

- **General allowances** can be applied to total receivables once they have any bad debts written off, or specific allowances deducted. In the case the company will use an average. Let's say Speed Ltd have £1m of debts due, but know on average 5% will not pay they might have a general allowance of £50,000.

General allowances using the aged receivables schedule

Example

One way to estimate a general allowances for receivables is to create an **aged receivables schedule**.

This is basically a list of receivables (amounts owed to a business) shown in order of how old they are, with a corresponding percentage that depends on their age.

This percentage shows how much of the total debts of that particular age are going to be considered 'doubtful'. The total of the 'doubtful' debts will then be allocated as an allowance to cover the potential bad debts.

Here is OBC's receivables age analysis:

Age of debt	Amount (£)	%	Allowance (£)
0 - 2 months	12,000	1	120
2 – 4 months	4,500	2	90
4 – 6 months	1,050	5	52.5
6+ months	210	20	42
	17,760		**304.5**

How do we account for an allowance for receivables? Like this:

Bad debts		
20X1 Allowance for receivables	304.5	

Allowance for receivables		
	20X1 Bad debts	304.5

So here we can see that the total allowance for receivables that may not ever get paid has been debited into the bad debts account to show it as an expense.

There is a corresponding liability in the allowance for receivables account.

At the end of the year, the bad debts account is credited to the income statement the bad debts account has effectively been closed off for that period.

Bad debts				
20X1	Allowance for receivables	304.5	31st Dec Income statement	304.5

Example – Change in allowance for receivables

Let's say that OBC's receivables allowance is decreased to £195 in the following year as they make fewer sales. They would account for this as follows:

Allowance for receivables			
20X2		20X2	
Bad debts	109.5	Balance b/d	304.5
Balance c/d	195.0		
	304.5		
		20X3	
		Balance b/d	195

Notice that there's a difference in the 20X1 and 20X2 balance of £109.50. Effectively too much was charged as a bad debt in 20X1 therefore and so it is reclaimed this year as income. A credit in an expense account is the same as income:

Bad debts			
		20X2	Allowance for receivables	109.5

astranti
financial training

CIMA BA3 Study Text

Chapter 8

Inventory

1. Inventory

What is inventory?

Inventory is all the stuff that makes up the basis of what your business sells or provides.

If you are a restaurant, your inventory will be the food and drinks; if you are a petrol station, your inventory is the petrol (and perhaps snacks and magazines, or whatever may be for sale in the shop); if you are a car dealership, your inventory is going to be cars.

According to the definition of IAS 2, which is the international accounting standard for inventories, **inventories are assets which are any one of the following:**

- **Held for sale in the ordinary course of business** – such as books in a bookshop

- **In the process of production for such sale** – such as cars in a car factory

- **In the form of material or supplies to be consumed in the production process or rendering of services** – such as cleaning equipment for a window cleaner

So, Jenny's inventory is the books which she sells in her shop. She doesn't manufacture books, and she doesn't use any other material or supplies in the process of selling her books.

So her inventory is simply the books she holds for sale in her shop.

Recording inventory

There are a few aspects to understanding inventory. One of the keys is distinguishing between opening inventory, purchases and closing inventory.

Jenny owns a bookshop where she sells all sorts of books. She needs to record changes in her inventory. Let's look at the changes in inventory at Jenny's bookshop to understand the differences.

Opening inventory

This is the **value of the inventory at the beginning of an accounting period.**

So, let's say Jenny opens her bookshop with 200 books. She purchased those books for £10 each, which means that all together her opening inventory is worth £2,000.

Purchases

This is the **amount spent on purchasing new inventory to be sold.** So, during the year, Jenny purchases 50 new books to sell to customers, for £10 each. Altogether, these purchases cost her £500.

So, her purchases would be £500.

Closing inventory

This is the **value of the remaining inventory at the end of the reporting period,** after accounting for purchases and sales.

Jenny sold 150 books in the year, so she would have 100 books left at the end of the year.

This is because she started of with 200, bought 50 and sold 150. 200 + 50 − 150 = 100.

We know that the books are worth £10 each, so the closing inventory amount is £1,000:

£10 x 100 = £1,000

2.   Measuring inventory

So, that's a simple example of how inventory works for an ordinary trading business. Let's now have a look at a manufacturing business.

Penny owns a factory where she makes chocolate bars, of which she then sells to resellers.

So, Penny's inventory not only includes the finished chocolate bars that she sells, but also all of the ingredients to make the chocolate bars that she has, as well as all the chocolate bars that are in the process of being made.

Measuring inventories

Under IAS 2, companies need to value their inventories as either of the following depending on which has the lowest value:

- **Cost**: This is the total cost incurred in getting the product to its current location and condition. So, this would include the purchase price of the ingredients as well as the cost of actually producing the chocolate from raw materials.

- **Net realisable value (NRV)**: This is the price at which the product is sold minus the cost of selling the item. It is also known as fair value. So, that would be the final price of the item less any costs for things such as delivery or packaging.

If the product's NRV is of a lower value than the cost, the inventory should be measured using that and not the cost. If the cost per item is lower than the NRV of the items, then the inventory should be valued using the cost.

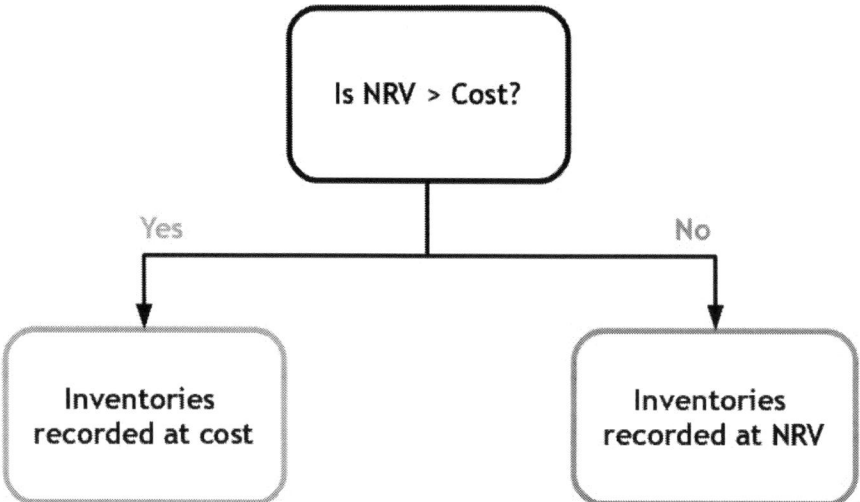

So, for example, let's look at Penny our chocolate factory owner.

The cost of a chocolate bar is 50p.

This is what it costs Penny to purchase the raw materials she uses to manufacture the chocolate bars including delivery prices.

It also includes the cost of actually producing the bars (electricity costs to run the machines, wages for staff who operate the machines).

The NRV of one of Penny's chocolate bars is the retail price (the price Penny sells a bar for) minus the 25p cost of packaging and delivery to the customer (the cost of selling):

£1 – 25p = 75p

So, the cost is 50p and the NRV is 75p. Therefore, we value a unit of inventory (one chocolate bar) at the cost price of 50p, because it is lower than the NRV of 75p.

Sometimes inventory will decrease in value.

For instance, if Jenny had some chocolate bars which were close to their sell by date, their retail price may decrease to 50p because they need to be sold quickly.

So now if we take away the cost of packaging and delivery, 25p, from the new retail price of 50p, then we are left with an NRV of 25p:

50p – 25p = 25p

This means that chocolate bars close to their sell by date would have to be valued according to their NRV of 25p.

Age of inventory

The age of the inventories will affect the total of the purchasing costs. This is because **the cost of the most recent items to have been purchased or produced will have been affected by inflation.**

So, if the most recent goods are sold first they will have a higher purchase cost relative to the selling price.

Therefore, before we workout the value of inventory we have to make an assumption regarding the relative age of the inventories we are valuing.

There are two main ways of doing this.

First in/First out (FIFO)

FIFO assumes that **items bought the longest time ago are the first to be sold.**

For example, Jenny had 5 of the first of the Harry Potter books in her store for which she paid £3, £5, £5, £6 and £7 respectively. Using a FIFO system, when she sells a book, it will be the £3 book that is sold.

This is assumed for cost purposes only, and is not an indication of stock rotation. i.e. it could have been any of the actual 5 books which were sold – for stock valuation purposes we'll assume it's the £3 book.

Last in/First out (LIFO)

This method, conversely to FIFO, assumes that **the most recently bought stock is the first to be sold.** Again, this is assumed for cost purposes only. In this case it's the £7 book which is the one sold, and £7 is used as the cost of the sale.

Using LIFO method tends to generate a higher cost of sales, and thus a lower gross profit. This is because items purchased most recently are affected by inflation, but may be sold at the same rate.

However, according to IAS 2, this is **not an acceptable method for financial accounting**. As such businesses do not generally use this method, but it is still possible that you might see an example in the exam where LIFO is used so you do need to be aware of it..

3. Components of cost

What makes something a cost for inventory? For example, say Penny bought ingredients for her chocolate bars.

The ingredients themselves were £500 and the delivery was £50. Is the cost of that chocolate bar £500 or is it now £550 because of the cost of delivery?

It is the latter, as delivery costs contribute towards the overall cost of the inventory, since this is money you had to spend directly on it in order to be able to sell it.

So let's take a closer look at what the components of cost are, and how to determine the cost of inventory.

Purchase costs

The purchase costs **include the price the items themselves cost, plus all the other costs of acquisitions** such as freight charges, customs duty, taxes not recoverable and fees paid for acquisition.

So, let's say Penny sells chocolate bars in the UK, and she needs to import a lot of her ingredients from foreign countries.

This is a breakdown of her purchases:

	£
Purchases	13,000
Freight charges	2,000
Customs duty	1,300
Non-recoverable tax	2,150
Total	**18,450**

And so her total purchase cost is £18,450, even though the cost of items alone was only £13,000.

Conversion costs

This refers to the costs incurred when a company produces goods within the business. Think of them as the costs incurred while converting the raw materials to finished products.

These costs include direct costs (direct labour and raw materials), **and also production overheads.**

Production overheads can be variable or fixed. **Variable production overheads are indirect costs that fluctuate** with the level of business activity, such as indirect materials (e.g. cleaning supplies, disposable safety equipment).

Fixed production overheads, on the other hand, **are indirect costs that remain the same** despite fluctuating levels of business activity, such as rental and insurance of a production warehouse.

Usually companies **work out a standard fixed overhead rate at the start of the financial year and use that to work out their fixed overhead.**

For example, if Jenny worked out that her fixed overhead rate for one chocolate bar was 25p and she produced 100,000 chocolate bars in a month her fixed overhead would be £25,000. If the next month she only produced 50,000 her fixed overhead for that month would be £12,500.

Financing costs

Financing costs are the **costs incurred by borrowing money to fund production or purchases**, such as interest on a loan.

Jenny took out a bank loan of £20,000 to pay for some new equipment. The loan has an interest rate of 10%, and so she will need to include a finance cost of £2,000.

Expenses not included in inventory valuation

The following costs are not to be included as part of the cost, but should rather be **treated as expenses** in the period they are incurred:

- **The cost of abnormal levels of wastage** – e.g. a machine malfunctions and produced a whole batch of units that are unusable

- **Costs for storage that are not related to the production process** – e.g. storing finished goods in a warehouse prior to sale is part of the production process, but storing a broken down machine until you can find a replacement is not

- **General administrative costs that are not related to production** – for instance, the cost of having the entire sales staff attend a training meeting

- **Selling and distribution costs** – e.g. the cost of managing the logistics of sales and delivery

Example

Jenny's chocolate factory incurred the following costs in the month of October. Her inventory has an estimated NRV of £30,000. Using the information below, calculate the total production cost for the period, and state at what value inventory should be recorded.

In the table below are the expenses for October at Jenny's chocolate factory:

	£
Raw materials	15,000
Direct labour costs	10,000
Associated consumables	8,000
Lighting and heating	6,000
Variable factory overheads	2,400
Administration costs	3,000
Selling and distribution costs	1,800
Depreciation of production equipment	1,200
Actual fixed overheads	7,000
Storage costs	1,150

Jenny's standard fixed overhead rate per chocolate bar is 25p.

Additional information:

- 80% of lighting and heating costs relate to production

- Administration costs are fixed, and of these 30% do not relate to production

- Storage costs are incurred when Jenny's goods are awaiting sale

- During the month 6,400 products were produced and half were left in stock at the end of the period. No stock remains from previous periods

Solution

First, we know that 80% of the lighting and heating costs related to production, and so we need to include this figure in the overall cost:

£6,000 x 80% = £4,800

Next, we must work out the fixed overhead costs. These should be based on the standard fixed overhead rate of 25p per chocolate bar (and not the actual amount spent). This means that fixed overhead costs for October were

25p x 6,400 = £1,600

Of the administration costs, 70% are related to production, giving:

70% of £3,000 = £2,100

So, let's put these figures into a table combined with the other production overheads which are shown in full:

	£
Raw materials	15,000
Direct labour costs	10,000
Associated consumables	8,000
Lighting and heating	4,800
Variable Factory overheads	2,400
Depreciation of production equipment	1,200
	41,400
Fixed factory overheads	1,600
Administration costs	2,100
Total cost	**45,100**

And so, we have a total cost of £45,100. This is how much it costs to get from the raw materials to finished goods.

Half of this stock remains so the value of stock is £22,550.

This is less than the NRV of £30,000, and so this should be the figure used to value inventory.

Disclosures for inventories

IAS 2 requires the following to be disclosed in the financial statements regarding inventories:

- The **accounting policies adopted** in measuring inventories, including the **cost formula used**

- The **total amount of inventories** in classifications appropriate to the business

- The **carrying amount of inventories which have been valued at net realisable value**

CIMA BA3 Study Text

Chapter 9

Non-current Assets

1. Assets

The general definition of **an asset is, 'something or someone of use or value'.** That's a good starting point, but we need to be more specific than that in financial reporting!

As we know, assets make up half of the balance sheet and are an important aspect of the accounting equation (Capital = Assets - Liabilities). But what counts as an asset? Let's try to get a clearer idea.

Tangible and intangible assets

So, you probably think you already know what an asset is; things like buildings, cars, cash, machinery are all assets. Well, that's true – these are known as tangible assets, but that's only half of the story.

In 1997, P. Diddy sampled the classic Police song, 'Every Breath You Take,' for a tribute track to his late best friend, Notorious B.I.G. called, 'I'll Be Missing You'. However, Diddy hadn't received legal permission to use the sample, which, had he done so, would have resulted in only having to give up 25% of the song royalties to Sting.

This meant that, unfortunately for Diddy (and fortunately for Sting, who owns 100% of the original), Diddy's carelessness to properly retain permission for the sample resulted in Sting reaping 100% of the royalties for the P. Diddy version.

To this day, Sting is reported to have earned between $20-$40 million for 'Every Breath You Take,' and at least $2,000 a day from P. Diddy's Grammy award winning, best selling single of all time, 'I'll Be Missing You.'

So, the copyright that Sting had for the song was obviously something of value, but is it an asset? The short answer is: yes. A copyright is an example of what we call an **intangible asset.** Intangible assets are **assets that do not have a physical presence.**

So, assets can be of two different types:

Tangible assets	Buildings, land, machines, inventories, cash.
Intangible assets	Copyrights, goodwill, patents, brands.

For this chapter we don't need to look at intangible assets and so we are only going to be interested in **tangible assets**. These are the main **physical assets** that we listed earlier; buildings, machinery, equipment, inventory, money, etc.

Current and non-current assets

Now, tangible assets may be further classified into sub-classes of either **non-current or current assets**.

Current assets

Current assets are assets that are **reasonably expected to be sold, consumed or used through the normal course of business operations within one year**. So, of the assets mentioned above, cash (currencies) and inventory (stock) are considered as tangible current assets, because they come in and go out of a business on a daily basis, and are thus **short-term**.

Non-current assets

In contrast, non-current assets are **long-term** and cannot easily be converted into cash within a short period of time. These assets are not normally sold directly to the consumers/end-users of an entity and instead go towards helping business operations. Typically, non-current assets are things that the company has for **12 months or longer**.

For example, a warehouse is a non-current asset, since it is a long-term store of the inventory (which will sell in the short-term). In this case, the warehouse will be used for as long as it is sufficient to the needs of the business, making it long-term (non-current).

However, the inventory will be sold and replenished whenever stock levels get low, making it short-term (current). So, from the above list, buildings, land and machines are examples of non-current tangible assets.

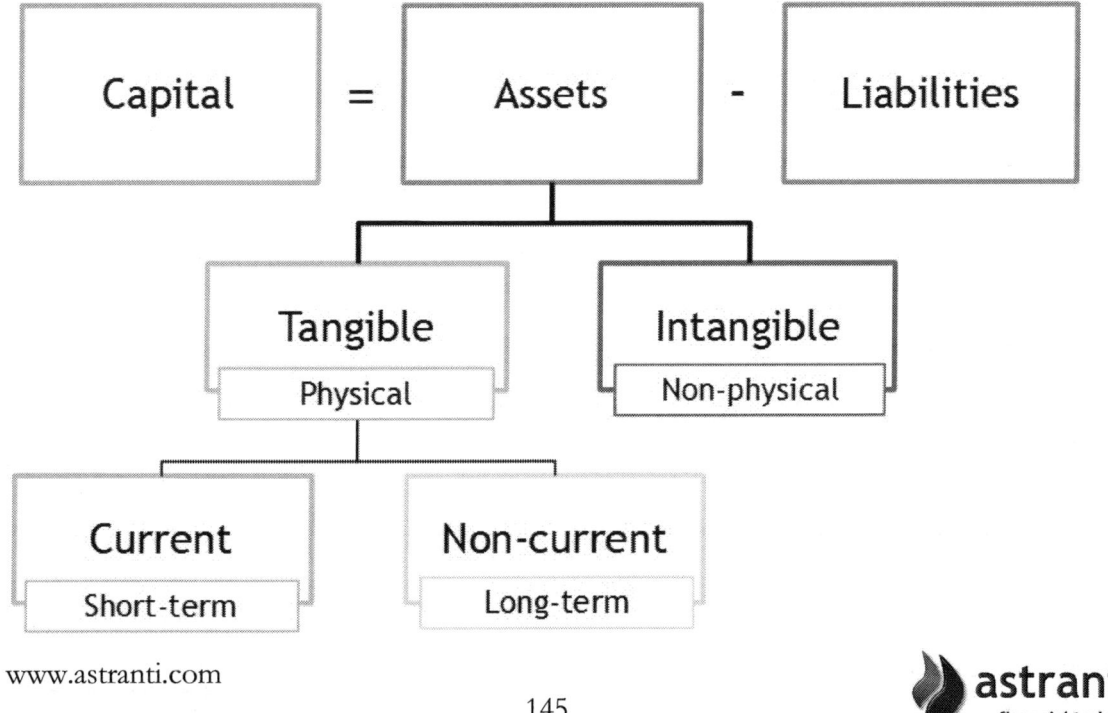

astranti
financial training

IAS 16 Property, Plant, and Equipment

Now we are ready to take a look at the formal definition for non-current assets (also known as fixed assets). The accounting standard relating to this is **IAS 16 Property, Plant and Equipment** (shortened to PP&E or PPE).

Now, for our purposes, Property, Plant and Equipment can be used interchangeably with non-current assets. This is because **all non-current assets fall into on of the categories of property, plant or equipment.**

For example, a building counts as property; plant refers to the kind of machinery that you may find in a factory, for example; and equipment is more general, including things like computers, phones, desks, etc.

Standard definition

Before we move on then, let's take a quick look at how IAS 16 defines PPE. **Property, plant and equipment are tangible assets that:**

- **are held by an entity for use in the production or supply of goods or services, for rental to others, or for administrative purposes, and;**

- **are expected to be used during more than one period**

Let's break down some of these key terms:

Aspect of definition	Explanation
'held by an entity for use'	This means it is used by the company in order to **help make money** rather than to be sold for money. e.g. A warehouse used to store inventory (property).
'production or supply of goods and services'	This means the asset **contributes to the main operations** of the company. e.g. Machinery used in production (plant).
'for rental to others'	This just means that **PPE can be leased to external parties** but it still needs to be shown in the financial statements of the owner. e.g. Renting out machinery for external use.
'for administrative purposes'	This refers to the **administrative needs of the company.** e.g. An office or office building (property).

Aspect of definition	Explanation
'used during more than one period'	This refers to the 'long-term' aspect of the asset, specifying that the **asset must be used over multiple periods**. e.g. A 5-year lease on a warehouse.

2. Capital and revenue

During the normal course of operation, a business will need to spend money in order to make money. This might be buying materials to transform into products, or it may be purchasing new machinery to increase production output. **These costs are actually quite different from an accounting perspective, and so we can distinguish two kinds of expenditure:**

Capital expenditure: This is **expenditure on non-current assets**, such as purchasing new land, buildings and equipment, since it is money spent on increasing the earning capabilities of the company in the future.

Revenue expenditure: This is **expenditure on current assets**, such as inventories, since it is money spent on keeping the company currently in business.

However, **when it comes to repairing, replacing or sometimes updating non-current assets, these costs are classified as revenue expenditure.** Let's see why this is the case with an example.

Example

Terry owns and runs a pub. Since the smoking ban, a lot of his regulars have been complaining that he doesn't have an outdoor smoking area and they have been using different pubs for this reason.

Terry also has a pool table in the pub, which was recently damaged and needs a new felt surface. So, Terry makes plans to invest in two things: a new outdoor smoking area for his pub and a new felt for his pool table. Which of these costs do you think is a capital expenditure? Which one is a revenue expenditure?

Well, clearly **the smoking area will be an asset that increases his potential customers. Therefore, this will be capitalised.**

And, since **the new felt on the pool table is just a repair, this is revenue expenditure**. However, let's suppose that with the repair of the felt, Terry was also given new pool balls, a new set of billiard and snooker balls (which he'd never had before) and a new range of pool cues.

Which of these does Terry classify as revenue and which as capital? Well, the felt, the pools balls and pool cues are essentially replacement, and so they are all revenue. However, the new billiard and snooker balls are brand new, and so they should be billed to capital expenditure.

3. Recognition (initial measurement)

Recognition criteria

Okay, so the classification is all done but this is financial reporting, so what we are really interested in is **how and when to record PPE in the accounts and financial statements**.

An asset is recognised in the financial statements if it fulfils **two criteria**:

- It is probable that any future **economic benefit** associated with the asset will **flow to or from the entity**; and,

- The asset has a **cost** or value that can be **measured reliably**.

Let's take a closer look at these criteria.

Economic benefit

It obviously makes sense for the entity to **only recognise an asset** as PPE **if the future economic benefit from its use becomes probable and will flow to the entity**.

For instance, going back to our warehouse example, we can ask whether this would meet the first criterion. To do so, we need to identify exactly what would be the economic benefit associated with the asset. This means identifying whether the **risk and rewards associated with the asset are transferred**.

What of our example?

- **Risk** - Well, the warehouse is a store of the inventory and so it keeps all of the products dry and safe and ready for sale. If there were a leak in the roof, the entity would be responsible for the damage caused to inventory and for repairing it.

- **Rewards** - The reward (or money) associated with this asset (the warehouse) will be from the sale of the inventory that it houses. In this case, the warehouse contains only the products that the entity sells, and so the reward (revenue from the sale of goods) will flow to the entity.

- So far so good, it's an asset we should recognise. We're not finished yet though.

Control

Another aspect of of this criteria is **establishing control**. Control of the asset **determines recognition**, and so it is very important to identify who controls and asset upfront. In our example, the entity is in control of the warehouse as the sole owner.

Indirect economic benefit

As you may have noticed from the example, the associated **economic benefit need not always be direct**. For instance, the warehouse itself was not directly making any money for the entity, but without it there would be nowhere to store inventory and so the warehouse indirectly contributes to the economic benefits of the company.

Cost

An important criterion for recognition is that **we should be able to reliably measure the cost of an asset**. Whether an asset has been purchased (which is the most likely scenario) or created by the company, there is a certain amount of cost attached to it.

Cost does not only mean invoice price. It also **includes amounts incurred to bring the asset to the location where it needs to be** and **condition the asset to become operational**. Attributable costs may also include **labour charges** to get the asset to its finished stage.

Example: purchased asset

FTP Ltd have just agreed to purchase machinery "A", which has been bought and shipped from overseas:

	£
Original cost (as per supplier's invoice)	50,000
Delivery of machinery from overseas to factory site	
Freight charges (for shipment of machinery)	1,400
Brokerage and handling fees	85
Import duties (for importing machinery)	2,500
Cartage (delivery of machinery to factory)	285
Preparation charges incurred	
Excavation charges (for site preparation)	2,300
Installation and machine assembly	1,000
Initial set-up and machinery testing	1,000
Staff training to operate machine	500
Total cost recognised for machinery "A"	59,070

All the expenditures listed above have been added to the total cost of the asset. This is because they all contributed in bringing the asset to its required location (the factory), as well as preparing the asset to be in a workable condition (assembly and set-up). Therefore, the total cost of £59,070 would be recorded as the cost of machinery "A" in the financial statements.

Example: produced asset

For assets that are created or produced by the company, the same concept applies. However, when it comes to non-current assets, it is less likely to be made in house.

Nonetheless, let's take the example of a computer manufacturer purchasing components to build personal computers that they also use in their office (which would come under equipment). The following components are bought to build a complete PC, with labour charges attributed to making one personal computer are also included:

	£
Original cost (as per supplier's invoice) -	
Monitor	30
Keyboard & Mouse	20
Housing and other parts	40
CPU and motherboard	70
Labour – component assembly	40
Total cost recognised for each PC	**200**

The total of £200 would be recognised as the cost of each personal computer in the financial statements.

4. Subsequent measurement

So let's imagine that we've bought a new piece of machinery for our company and we've got as far as recognition (or initial measurement) in the books. We've identified that it is a long-term asset from which (indirect) economic benefits are expected to flow and we've also calculated an initial cost of £40,000:

Debit	PPE	£40,000	
Credit	Bank		£40,000

PPE			
Bank	£40,000		

Now it's a year later and you wonder how the asset now needs to be shown in the financial statements. Do we use the same figure as last year or do we need to find an up to date market price (or the 'fair value')?

Well, it turns out that the decision is up to you! Non-current assets can be subsequently measured using either the **cost model** or the **revaluation model.**

Historic cost model

Simply put, under the cost model (or sometimes know as the **historic cost model**), **assets are recorded by the amount paid (or consideration given) for them at the time of their acquisition.** Even if the fair value of an asset significantly increases afterwards, the entity will continue to use the historic cost as the basis of measuring the asset. Depreciation and impairment losses are the only adjustments made in this model (more on these later).

So, the machinery that was purchased had an initial cost of £40,000. A year later, based on the fair value of the asset in the current market the machinery is now worth £42,000. However, if the company is using the cost model as its accounting policy, the subsequent measurement for the machinery in the financial statements will remain at the historic cost of £40,000.

Revaluation model

The revaluation model is when **the asset is subsequently recorded at fair value (the re-valued amount).** The re-valued amount, then, is the fair value of an asset at revaluation date, less subsequent depreciation and impairment (again, more on these later). Initially, **the asset is still initially recorded using its original cost.** It is only subsequently that any movement in fair value will need to be recognised.

Let us take the previous example of the machinery with historic cost of £40,000. A year later, the asset is re-valued and found to now have a fair value of £42,000. If the company chooses the revaluation model as its accounting policy, then the additional increase of £2,000 would need to be recorded.

Increase in value

If the value increases, the added amount is recognised in 'other comprehensive income' (this is a section of the Income Statement) as **"revaluation reserve"**. With our previous example, the entries will be as follows:

Debit	PPE	£2,000	
Credit	Revaluation reserve (I/S)		£2,000

PPE			
B/f	£40,000		
Revaluation reserve	£2,000	C/f	£42,000
	£42,000		£42,000
B/d	£42,000		

Revaluation reserve			
Income statement	£2,000	PPE	£2,000

Income Statement			
		Revaluation reserve	£2,000

Decrease in value

However, if the value decreases, the difference will **only be recorded in other comprehensive income** provided there is a balance in the revaluation reserve account to cover it.

As an example, lets say the machinery is re-valued at £39,000, a decrease. Also, there is currently nothing in the revaluation reserve account. The company, using the revaluation model, will then need to make the following transaction entries:

Debit	Loss on revaluation (Income Statement)	£1,000	
Credit	PPE		£1,000

PPE			
B/f	£40,000	Loss on revaluation	£1,000
		C/f	£39,000
	£40,000		£40,000
B/d	£39,000		

Income Statement	
Loss on revaluation	£1,000

The loss on revaluation is immediately recognised as an expense since there is no balance in the revaluation reserve account to offset.

If there is an **insufficient balance** in the revaluation reserve account, then **the difference will offset the account balance first**, and the rest is then expensed in the income statement.

Once again, let us use the same example, but this time, we assume a credit balance of £400 in the revaluation reserve account related to this property. The entries will be shown as follows:

Debit	Revaluation reserve	£400
Debit	Income statement (Loss on revaluation)	£600
Credit	PPE	£1,000

The credit balance in the revaluation reserve account is cleared first. Then the remaining loss is expensed. Here is the same process in the individual accounts:

PPE			
B/f	£40,000	Income statement	£600
		Revaluation reserve	£400

Revaluation reserve			
PPE	£400	B/f	£400

Income Statement		
PPE	£600	

When to re-value

Although the frequency of revaluation is not specified, the company will be required to undertake valuation on a **regular basis** (usually annually). This way, the carrying amount reflected for the asset will always include any increase (or decrease) in value.

When doing subsequent measurements using the revaluation model, **the fair value** of land and building should be market-related and should be **appraised by a professional**.

Of course, all this is a bit of a hassle, particularly if you had a lot of assets to value each year; as a result many companies prefer the historic cost model.

5. Depreciation

Introduction

So far, so good, but there is one major aspect of accounting for non-current assets that we've not yet looked at: depreciation. In simple terms, depreciation is **how we include the cost of an asset in the accounts over time**. Let's consider an example to understand why we do this.

Imagine that a company needs to buy a brand new machine for their factory due to a recent increase in demand that the current facilities can't keep up with. The new machine will cost £300,000, but the company has only been making around £500,000 in revenue each year, and so if we include the entire cost of the machinery in the year in which it is purchased it will significantly reduce profit for the year (perhaps even causing a loss). However, in the following year the profits will shoot back up again since there is no extra cost to include:

	Year 1 (£)	Year 2 (£)
Revenue	500,000	510,000
Cost of new machinery	(300,000)	-
Other costs	(250,000)	(265,000)
Profit/(loss)	(50,000)	245,000

In addition, charging the entire cost of the machinery at once doesn't really make sense because the asset will presumably last for several years. Therefore, spreading that cost out over the time that the asset is expected to be useful (its 'useful life') gives a better representation of how the cost of the asset is 'absorbed' by the company. And that is precisely what depreciation is: is **the systematic reduction of the value of a tangible asset over its useful life**.

So, going back to our example, **we would estimate the useful life of the machinery (that's just how long we can expect it to be useful) and spread the cost over that many years**. So, if we use a useful life of 4 years we would get an annual depreciation charge of £75,000 (£300,000 ÷ 4):

	Year 1 (£)	Year 2 (£)	Year 3 (£)	Year 4 (£)
Revenue	500,000	510,000	525,000	540,000
Depreciation	(75,000)	(75,000)	(75,000)	(75,000)
Other costs	(250,000)	(265,000)	(270,000)	(275,000)
Profit/loss	175,000	170,000	180,000	190,000

As you can see, this method gives a far more **accurate portrayal of the company's financial activity**, which is ultimately the key function of financial reporting!

Depreciation: Key ideas

Before we get into the specifics of accounting for depreciation, let's just formalise and define some of the ideas we've just considered:

Useful life

Useful life refers to **the duration that an asset will be purposeful to the business**. Most tangible assets have useful lives that are limited between **2 to 20 years** and all these assets are subject to depreciation. However, it does not always correspond with how long the asset will actually last.

After all, a computer could physically last for 20 years (albeit it might become slow and cumbersome as it "grows" older). But due to the speed of technological advancement and changes, the computer might only be truly useful for 3 years. Therefore, 3 years, not 20, is considered as the useful life of the computer.

The useful life of an asset should be **periodically reviewed by the company** (normally around balance sheet date). This way, any significant changes on future depreciation charges can be adjusted.

Residual value

Residual value is **how much an asset will be worth at the end of its useful life**. This is also known as the 'salvage value' or scrap value. The residual value of an asset can generally be estimated using an agreement or appraisal.

Any estimated cost related to the disposal of an asset (for instance, the cost of removal or demolishing) can be deducted from its residual value.

If an asset has a residual value, then the residual value will be the lowest amount to which that said asset can be depreciated.

As an example, let us take a motor vehicle with a cost of £3,000 and has a useful life of 5 years. This vehicle can be sold back to the car dealership or used as a deposit for a new one at the end of its useful life. The agreed upon residual value is £400. There would also be a collection fee of £50 (when the dealership collects the vehicle).

The residual value of the vehicle will be £350 (£400 less collection fee of £50). The depreciable amount of £2,650 (cost £3,000 less calculated residual value of £350) will be depreciated over 5 years, giving a charge of £530 per year:

	Year 1 (£)	Year 2 (£)	Year 3 (£)	Year 4 (£)	Year 5 (£)
Book Value	3,000	2,470	1,940	1,410	880
Depreciation	(530)	(530)	(530)	(530)	(530)
Carry value	2,470	1,940	1,410	880	**350**

The depreciation charge

The depreciation charge is shown as **an expense in the profit and loss statement**. Companies depreciate assets for accounting and tax purposes.

Depreciation **starts as soon as the asset has reached the location and working condition it requires.**

For example, say an office space was bought by a company at the start of the year, in January, for the purpose of relocating its sales department. This office space required revamping (fitting walls and doors, etc.) so that it could become a safe, free and work-friendly environment. In June of the same year, the renovations were finally completed and the sales department moved into the office space. Depreciation would therefore only commence in June since that is the time the office space started becoming useful to the company.

6. Calculating depreciation

When it comes to calculating how much an asset has depreciated in a given accounting period, there are two main methods used:

- **The straight-line method**

- **The reducing-balance method**

IAS 16 requires that the **depreciation method used should reflect the pattern in which the asset's economic benefits are consumed** by the entity. For instance, assets that are 'used up' more in earlier years and less later on (such as a machine that deteriorates and becomes less productive over time) need to be depreciated in a way that reflects that usage.

The straight-line method

Using the straight-line method, the **depreciation is calculated by charging an equal amount of the cost of the asset to each accounting period during the asset's useful life**. This is the kind of depreciation we've looked at in our examples so far.

When presented on a graph, the depreciation amount appears as a straight line, which is where the name comes from.

Formula

The depreciation is calculated using the following formula:

$$\text{Depreciation per annum} = \frac{\text{Original cost} - \text{Estimated residual value}}{\text{Estimated useful life}}$$

Useful life can be in days, months or years, but you have to be consistent. Usually, though, depreciation is calculated over several years.

Example

Terry owns and runs a pub. Since his government imposed a smoking ban in pubs, a lot of his regulars have been complaining that he doesn't have an outdoor smoking area and they have been using different pubs for this reason. So, Terry makes plans to invest in a new outdoor smoking area for his pub. Since the smoking area would count as property, it will be recognised as a non-current asset and needs to be depreciated.

The smoking area is not the kind of thing that is 'used up' more in earlier years, so we will use the straight line method of depreciation. The relevant figures are as follows:

Cost of the smoking area (as of 01st Jan 20X1)	£13,750
Estimated useful life	10 years
Estimated residual value	£500

So, putting these numbers into the equation gives us:

$$\text{Depreciation per annum} = \frac{£13,750 - £500}{10} = £1,325$$

So, in the statement of financial position, the carrying amount is reduced by **£1,325** every year. In the income statement, this amount is charged as an expense and subtracted from the profits. Here is how we calculate the carrying amount for the statement of financial position:

		Cost	Acc. Depreciation	Carrying amount
20X1	Non-current assets	£13,750	£1,325	£12,425
20X2	Non-current assets	£13,750	£2,650	£11,100
20X3	Non-current assets	£13,750	£3,975	£9,775
20X4	Non-current assets	£13,750	£5,300	£8,450
20X5	Non-current assets	£13,750	£6,625	£7,125
20X6	Non-current assets	£13,750	£7,950	£5,800
20X7	Non-current assets	£13,750	£9,275	£4,475
20X8	Non-current assets	£13,750	£10,600	£3,150
20X9	Non-current assets	£13,750	£11,925	£1,825
20Y0	Non-current assets	£13,750	£13,250	£500

You'll notice in this table, that we accumulate depreciation on this asset year by year by adding on the current charge to the balance at the start of each year. This is called accumulated depreciation.

Accumulated depreciation is removed from the cost of an asset during workings in the statement of financial position, leaving the asset's carrying amount in the statement.

The non-current asset account will therefore show the cost of the asset. The asset's cost in this account will only change if it is re-valued at a later date.

Smoking Area		
Jan X1	Bank	£13,750

Accumulated depreciation is not charged to the individual asset accounts and is instead credited to an accumulated depreciation account. This effectively reduces the cost of the asset to its carry value on the statement of financial position.

Accumulated depreciation					
Dec X1	Balance c/d	£1,325	Dec X1	Depreciation	£1,325
		£1,325			£1,325
			Jan X2	Balance b/d	£1,325
Dec X2	Balance c/d	£2,650	Dec X2	Depreciation	£1,325
		£2,650			£2,650

At the end of X1, the carrying value of the asset is £13,750 - £1,325 = £12,2425. One year later it is £13,750 - £2,650 = £11,100. The value gradually reduces in the accounts over the life of the asset.

The annual depreciation charge is an expense for a specific accounting period. At the end of the year the depreciation expense account is closed off, with the expense charged to the statement of profit loss and presented in the income statement.

Depreciation					
Dec X1	Acc. Dep	£1,325	Dec X1	P&L	£1,325

The reducing-balance method

Sometimes, assets won't depreciate by the same amount each period and so we can't use the straight-line method. What happens with these assets is that they **depreciate more early on and less when they are older**.

This is usually the case with assets that have a higher production or value making rate when they are new (imagine production line equipment that can produce 100 items an hour when new, but after time can only produce 50 items an hour).

When this is the case we use the reducing-balance method. This is where **a constant percentage of depreciation is applied to the remaining proportion of the asset yet to be depreciated**. The way we spread the cost reflects the output of the asset over time. On a graph the depreciation charge would appear as a downwards sloping curve.

Formula

Reducing-balance depreciation is calculated using the following formula:

Depreciation per annum =   (Original cost – Acc. Depreciation)   x Rate %

The rate of depreciation is defined according to the estimated pattern of an asset's use over its life term. You don't need to worry about how it is calculated for now as it will always be given to you in a question if you are required to use the reducing balance method.

Example

Taking the same figures as before – but let's assume that Terry invests in an asset that depreciates more at the start, and less at the end. Let's say the rate of annual depreciation is 31%.

	£	
Original cost	13,750.00	
Year 1 depreciation	4,262.50	(13,750.00 x 0.31)
	9,487.50	
Year 2 depreciation	2,941.13	(9,487.50 x 0.31)
	6,546.37	

When the useful life of the asset is over (end of life) all that should remain is the estimated residual value.

When it comes to recording the data in the ledger and financial statements, we can do it in the same way as we did for the straight-line method, but with the appropriate changes:

Accumulated depreciation

Dec X1	Balance c/d	£4,262.50	Dec X1	Depreciation	£4,262.50
		£4,262.50			£4,262.50
			Jan X2	Balance b/d	£4,262.50
Dec X2	Balance c/d	£7,203.63	Dec X2	Depreciation	£2,941.13
		£7,203.63			£7,203.63

Depreciation

Dec X1	Acc. Dep	£4,262.50	Dec X1	P&L	£4,262.50
Dec X2	Acc. Dep	£2,941.13	Dec X1	P&L	£2,941.13

The carrying amount (or Net Book Value) at the end of each year is as follows:

		Cost	Acc. Depreciation	Carrying amount
20X1	Non-current assets	£13,750	£4,262.50	£9,487.50
20X2	Non-current assets	£13,750	£7,203.63	£6,546.37

7. De-recognition

Introduction

De-recognition deals with the **retirement or disposal of an asset**. It is the **removal of an asset from an entity's statement of financial position**. An asset is usually de-recognised because it has been donated, scraped or sold, for instance, if a company invests in new machinery, which leaves the old machinery available for sale.

De-recognition also takes place when an entity's **contractual right to an asset and its future economic benefits has expired**. For example, if you owned a warehouse, but in the contract ownership passes on to another person after 5 years, at the end of the 5th year you would need to remove it from the accounts/statements.

Gain and loss on disposal

Gains and losses on the disposal of an asset arise when there is **a difference between the proceeds received and the net carrying value of an asset at the date of disposal.**

astranti
financial training

Any gains or losses with regards to the disposal are **recognised in the profit and loss statement** as either income or expense. Gains on the disposal of asset cannot be classified as revenue because this transaction falls outside of the primary activities of an entity.

Example

Machinery which was originally purchased for £10,000 has accumulated depreciation of £6,200 and so had a net carrying amount of £3,800. This machinery was sold for £4,000.

This means the selling company made a gain of £200 (£4,000 - £3,800) on the sale of the asset.

The entries will be recorded as follows:

Firstly we recognise the money received from the bank (and increase in an asset is a debit – **DeAd** clic)

Bank		
Disposal	£4,000	

We put the credit into a 'disposal account' which groups together everything related to the sale and helps us calculate the profit or loss on sale.

Disposal		
	Bank	£4,000

Next we need to take the asset out of the machinery account where it was originally recorded at it's cost. To put an asset in is a debit (**DeAd** clic) and so to take it out must be the other side of the account i.e. a credit:

Machinery		
	Disposal	£10,000

And the other side of the double entry also goes to the disposal account:

Disposal			
Machinery	£10,000	Bank	£4,000

So that's the asset removed from the machinery account, but the accumulated depreciation is still in the books. Let's remove that:

Accumulated depreciation		
Disposal	£6,200	

The other side of the double entry again goes to the disposal account which can now be balanced to find the profit or loss on disposal:

Disposal

Machinery	£10,000	Bank	£4,000
Profit (income st.)	£200	Acc. depreciation	£6,200
	£10,200		£10,200

So we see here our £200 profit which is taken to the profit and loss statement and then on to the income statement as a gain in the period.

Revaluation reserve

If an asset to be disposed of was previously re-valued, **any surplus recorded in the revaluation reserve associated with said asset can be transferred directly to the retained earnings**.

We do this because we are essentially 'closing down' the revaluation reserve associated with the asset and relocating the balance to retained earnings (which are the accumulated profits of the entity). This transfer should also be included in the statement of changes in equity.

Let us take the same situation as above with the sold machinery, but imagine that £2,000 of the asset value was actually due to an upwards revaluation of the asset in the past. The double entry for that will look like this:

Revaluation reserve

Retained earnings	£2,000	B/f	£2,000
		Balance	£0

Retained earnings

		Revaluation reserve	£2,000

We've been using DEAD CLIC a lot to help us with our double entry, but rarely have we used the two C's. That's Credit and Capital. Here's a nice example of that though. Increasing a capital account (retained earnings) is a credit!

Disposal via part exchange

Sometimes, the value of an old asset goes towards the purchase price of a replacement asset, in what is know as a part exchange agreement (PEA). For example, if a new machine costs £50,000, you may exchange an old machine worth £15,000 and pay the difference of £35,000 in cash.

The accounting process is similar to a regular disposal.

1. Record the cash payment

Firstly let's account for the cash payment portion. This is exactly the same as we saw when there was a payment in full:

Machinery		
Bank	£35,000	

Bank		
	Machinery	£35,000

2. Record the part exchange value

Notice that so far we have £35,000 of assets recorded but that the value of the machine is £50,000. We need another debit of £15,000 to recognise the full value of the asset:

Machinery		
Machinery	£35,000	
Disposal	£15,000	

The credit is taken to a disposal account:

Disposal		
	Machinery	£15,000

Now the full £50,000 is recognised in the asset account.

3. Take the old machine out of the accounts and recognise and gain/loss on disposal

Let's say the old machine cost £40,000 originally, and had accumulated depreciation on it of £30,000, meaning its net book value was £10,000.

When it's part exchanged for £15,000, a £5,000 profit has been made. We therefore need to recognise the profit as well as take the asset out of the cost and accumulated depreciation accounts. Here's the relevant double entry:

Take out the old machine from the machinery account (credit)

Machinery			
Machinery	£35,000	Disposal	£40,000
Disposal	£15,000		

Take out the accumulated depreciation from the accumulated depreciation account (a debit):

Accumulated depreciation	
Machinery	£30,000

Put the other side of the double entries into the disposal account and balance to find the profit or loss:

Disposal			
Machinery	£40,000	Machinery	£15,000
Profit (income state.)	£5,000	Acc. depreciation	£30,000
	£45,000		£45,000

And we find there is £5,000 balance as we'd expect which is taken to the profit and loss account and then on to the income statement.

8. Comprehensive example

Let's pull all this together to do an all-inclusive question...

Company PP specialises in the manufacture of plumbing pipes. 5 years ago, the company decided to purchase machinery C to help in its production. Machinery C had a cost price of £80,000 and was supplied by an overseas vendor.

Recognition/Initial measurement

With its delivery, machinery C attracted import duties of £4,000 and transport cost of £2,500 to get it to the factory. Moreover, machinery C required setting up and assembly, which cost the company a further £1,500.

Solution

Let's start by calculating the cost, since it's already been established in the question that machinery C is a non-current asset (PPE). Remember that the total cost will include associated costs of getting the asset to the location and condition in which in needs to be:

Cost price	£80,000
Import duties	£4,000
Transport cost	£2,500
Set-up/assembly	£1,500
Total cost	£88,000

Subsequent measurement and depreciation calculation

Machinery C started operating the same year in which it was purchased. It had an expected useful economic life of 15 years.

From the outset, Company PP selected to adopt the revaluation model as its accounting policy and in year 3, the asset is revalued at £90,000. They also use a 25% reducing balance depreciation method.

Solution

Okay, so we need to calculate the depreciation for 5 years using a reducing-balance rate of 25%. Let's start with just the first year:

Year 1:

Cost price	£88,000	
Less: depreciation	(£22,000)	(£88,000 x 25%)
Net carrying amount	£66,000	

astranti
financial training

So, here we have started with the total cost of £88,000 that we calculated in the previous question. Next we need to calculate the depreciation charge. The reducing-balance formula is:

Depreciation per annum =   (Original cost – Residual value)   x Rate %

But since there is no mention of a residual value in the question, we should assume it is £0 (even though the asset will probably end up with a positive carry value). Therefore, depreciation is £88,000 x 25% = £22,000.

So that is the basic idea, let's see how that's done in the accounts. So, the asset account will always show the cost value of the asset. We also have a corresponding accumulated depreciation account and the combination of these two accounts give us the carry value of the asset:

Machinery	
Cost	£88,000

We also need to make entries regarding the depreciation:

Depreciation	
Machinery C	£22,000

Depreciation is an expense, so this is a debit (DEad clic). It is then added as a credit to the accumulated depreciation account:

Acc. Depreciation	
	Depreciation £22,000

So the balance of the asset account less the balance of the accumulated depreciation will equal the carrying value of the asset:

£88,000 - £22,000 = £66,000.

Year 2:

We can follow the same ideas in year 2:

Net carrying amount from year 1	£66,000	
Less: depreciation	(£16,500)	(£66,000 x 25%)
Net carrying amount	£49,500	

And in the accounts:

astranti
financial training

Machinery

Balance b/d	£88,000	Balance c/d	£88,000
	£88,000		£88,000
Balance b/d	£88,000		

Depreciation

Machinery C	£16,500		

Acc. Depreciation

		Balance b/d	£22,000
Balance c/d	£38,500	Depreciation	£16,500
	£38,500		£38,500

£88,000 - £38,500 = £49,500.

Year 3:

Okay, so we know from the question that company PP are using the revaluation model for subsequent measurement. Revaluation occurs every 3 years, and so we need to record the revaluation in year 3. This means that we will need to set up a revaluation reserve for the change in value of the asset.

Now, since the asset has been revalued to £90,000, we need to first record the increase in the asset account.

We'll balance that account off while we're at it:

Machinery

Balance b/d	£88,000		
Revaluation reserve	£2,000	Balance c/d	£90,000
	£90,000		£90,000
Balance b/d	£90,000		

And also show this in the revaluation reserve:

Revaluation reserve

		Machinery	£2,000

astranti
financial training

We also need to deal with the accumulated depreciation on the asset. Since the asset at cost has increased by £2,000, we need to add back the amount that was depreciated in years 1 and 2.

We do this by debiting the accumulated depreciation account and crediting the revaluation reserve:

Acc. Depreciation

Revaluation reserve	£38,500	Balance b/d	£38,500
	£38,500		£38,500

Revaluation reserve

		Machinery	£2,000
		Acc. Depreciation	£38,500

And balancing the revaluation reserve gives us:

Revaluation reserve

		Machinery C	£2,000
Balance c/d	£40,500	Acc. Depreciation	£38,500
	£40,500		£40,500
		Balance b/d	£40,500

Since the asset was revalued in year 3, there is no need to depreciate it, since the revalued amount is an accurate estimate of its carry value.

Notice that the total in the revaluation reserve is the £90,000 revaluation less the £49,500 carrying value at the start of the year (= £40,500).

Year 4:

So now, the cost of the asset is £90,000 and we can continue depreciating it as usual.

Machinery C in year 3	£90,000	
Less: depreciation	(£22,500)	(£90,000 x 25%)
Net carrying amount	£67,500	

Year 5:

Net carrying amount from year 4	£67,500	
Less: depreciation	(£16,875)	(£67,500 x 25%)
Net carrying amount	£50,625	

De-recognition

At the end of year 5, company PP decided to decommission machinery C and replace it with a new machine. A local scrap dealer has agreed to buy machinery C for £54,000.

Firstly, we debit the bank account with the proceeds of the disposal:

Bank			
Disposal	£54,000		

We then put the credit into a disposal account which groups together everything related to the sale and helps us calculate the profit or loss on sale.

Disposal			
		Bank	£54,000

Next we need to take the asset out of the machinery account where it was originally recorded at its cost:

Machinery			
Balance b/f	£90,000	Disposal	£90,000

And the other side of the double entry also goes to the disposal account:

Disposal			
Machinery	£90,000	Bank	£54,000

So that's the asset removed from the machinery account, but the accumulated depreciation is still in the books. Remember that we cleared the accumulated depreciation account when we revalued the asset in year 3, so we just need to count the depreciation since the revaluation. Depreciation for years 3 and 4 were £22,500 and £16,875 respectively, giving a total accumulated depreciation of £39,375:

Accumulated depreciation			
Disposal	£39,375	Balance b/f	£39,375

The other side of the double entry again goes to the disposal account, which can now be balanced to find the profit or loss on disposal:

Disposal			
Machinery	£90,000	Bank	£54,000
Profit (income st.)	£3,375	Acc. depreciation	£39,375
	£93,375		£93,375

So we see here our £3,375 profit, which is taken to the profit and loss statement and then on to the income statement as a gain in the period.

Revaluation reserve

So, finally, we need to transfer the balance of the revaluation reserve to retained earnings. In year 3 we set up the revaluation reserve and it ended up with a balance of £40,500. This shows the increase from machinery C's value in year 2 of £49,500 to £90,000 in year 3. All we do now is debit the reserve and credit the retained earnings (a capital account):

Revaluation reserve			
Retained earnings	£40,500	Balance b/d	£40,500

Retained earnings			
		Revaluation reserve	£40,500

9. Non-current asset register

Imagine a company such as Ford Motors and how many non-current assets they have. The buildings, property, land, machines, factories, robots et al. That's a lot of stuff! How on earth do they keep track of it all?

Well, entities have what is called a non-current asset register, which is **a list of all of a company's non-current assets**. It's essential insofar that it enables entities to keep tabs on and control their assets. Here's an example of what a non-current asset register might look like:

Asset No.	Description	Date acquired	Cost (£)	Acc. Dep (£)	Carry value (£)
1823	Central office	02/05/X4	250,450	75,135	175,315
1824	Storage depot	15/01/X7	45,000	3,375	41,625
1825	Equip - Laptop	08/08/X6	550	440	110
1826	Furniture - Desk	09/08/X6	249	199	50

As you can see, the assets have:

- Unique codes
- The date of acquisition
- Historic cost
- Accumulated depreciation
- Carry value

An asset register may contain more columns, such as:

- Depreciation method used
- Current location
- Estimated useful life

Or any other relevant information that may be useful to managers to help them make decisions about assets.

CIMA BA3 Study Text

Chapter 10

Intangible Assets

1.   IAS 38 Intangible Assets

Introduction

Okay, so we know what a tangible asset is: physical things such as property, plant, and equipment, inventory or money. How about other kinds of assets that aren't so obvious? How about things like copyrights, a company's reputation, or a brand? These things are controlled by, and make money for, a company, but aren't so easy to quantify financially.

Definition

According to IAS 38 Intangible Assets, an intangible asset can be described as **"an identifiable non-monetary asset without physical substance. It is a resource that is controlled by the entity as a result of past events and from which future economic benefits are expected"**:

- **Without physical substance** - The most defining characteristic of an intangible asset is that it does not have any physical presence. Intangibles cannot be felt or touched, e.g. a patent.

- **A resource controlled by the entity** - It is also important to determine if the benefits to be derived from the intangible assets are in the **control** of the company. For example, in pop music there is often an issue over copyright when songs are covered or sampled. This can be further obscured by artists not owning their own copyright, instead having them owned and controlled by record companies or external parties.

- **Future economic benefits** - Future economic benefits from the intangible asset must be **evident and probable**. For example, a patent for a ground breaking new technology is likely to yield future economic benefits, whereas the patent for a charcoal flavoured drink is unlikely to be fruitful.

The value of intangibles

Intangible assets can prove to be extremely valuable to the company, as often they provide **market advantage**. They have critical impact on the long-term success or failure of a business. And so, while tangible assets increase the company's current worth, **intangibles have more to do with increasing the company's future worth**.

However, like goodwill and brand name recognition, intangibles can easily be destroyed by excessive **carelessness** and **bad reputation**.

The oil company, British Petroleum (BP), is a well-known example of how easy it is for business reputations to be damaged, and how difficult they can be to rebuild. BP's

reputation was damaged by prolonged bad publicity about the Deepwater Horizon oil spill, causing their share price to drop by half over a period of 2 months.

However, BP has been pro-active. Since the accident, BP informs the public regularly about its remedial efforts with regards to the oil spill. This action has somewhat curbed BP's negative image.

Definite intangibles

Definite intangibles are assets that are **contract-based** with an agreed-upon expiration date. They have a **limited lifespan**.

An example of a definite intangible asset is the cross-licensing deal on technology patent between Samsung Electronics and Google Inc. In January 2014, Samsung and Google, which are primary backers of the Android mobile operating system, have decided to strengthen their positions in the smartphone market. Their agreement does not transfer ownership of patents between the two companies. Instead, the companies hope to improve collaboration on research and development of current and future products over the next 10 years.

Indefinite intangibles

Indefinite intangibles are assets that **do not have limiting factors** to their useful life. Most of the time, these assets are not amortised as there is no foreseeable limit to the benefit or cash flow generated from them.

A simple example of an indefinite intangible asset would be the brand name of a company (perhaps something like the Big Mac at McDonald's). The brand name would stay with the company for as long as the company continues operation and wishes to use the brand name.

2. Recognition

Recognition criteria

Similar to their tangible counterparts, intangible assets are recognised if they satisfy the following criteria:

- It is probable that any **future economic benefit** associated with the asset will **flow to or from the entity**; and

- The asset has a **cost or value** that can be **measured reliably**

Intangible assets are required to fulfil the basic recognition criteria regardless of whether they were acquired externally or generated internally. There are additional recognition criteria for internally generated intangible assets.

If an intangible item **fails to meet both recognition criteria**, IAS 38 dictates that the said item must then be **recorded as an expense** in the financial statement when it is incurred. Once an item has been expensed, it **cannot be re-instated** as an intangible asset.

Economic benefit

According to IAS 38, the probability of future economic benefits from intangible assets may be based on **reasonable** and **supportable assumptions** about conditions that will exist over the life of the asset.

Simply put, it means that there is an exceptionally high likelihood of gaining benefit from the asset. It also means that the assessment and estimation of this likelihood must be supported by available information, preferably from external evidences.

Copyright and film rights on the next book to be written by a famous author would be examples of intangible assets with a good likelihood of future benefits.

Cost

A main criterion for recognition is that we should be able to reliably measure the cost of an asset. The cost of an intangible asset is measured in the same way as we would measure a tangible asset.

Cost includes the **price a company pays** for the asset, as well as **amounts incurred to condition the asset into working order**. With purchased intangibles, cost price would normally be the fair value of the asset at the time of procurement.

Sometimes it will happen that intangible assets are purchased as part of a business acquisition. Basically, aside from intangibles, there would also be purchased goodwill in the transaction. If at all possible, the cost of the intangible assets and goodwill must be separately recognised. This is because the users of financial statements need to be able to distinguish between goodwill and something like a patent.

Goodwill

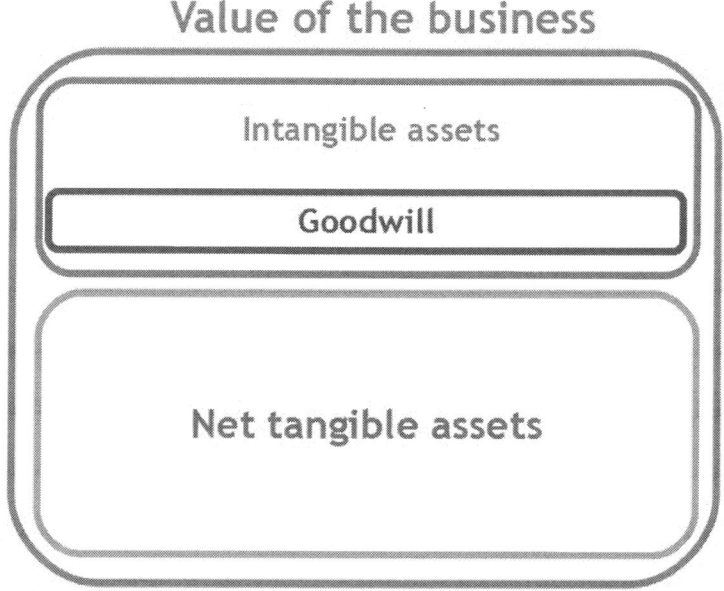

In the image above we have a rough break down of what makes up the value of a company. Starting at the bottom we have the net tangible assets, which will usually make up the majority of the company's value. Above that we have the intangible assets, which as we know include the non-physical assets. One intangible asset in particular that we ought to draw attention to is goodwill.

Goodwill is the **economic value placed on the reputation and image of an entity**. For instance, let's say you are going to buy a company. The fair value of their net assets (that is the market price for all of their assets less the cost of their liabilities) may be £1,000,000, but you may decide to offer over and above that amount in recognition of the good reputation and image of the company. So you decide to offer £1,200,000, where the extra £200,000 is considered to be goodwill.

Goodwill can be acquired externally (purchased) or generated internally:

- **Purchased goodwill** would normally involve a merger or acquisition with another entity (such as in the above example).

- **Internally generated goodwill** is, as the term implies, created by the company. For instance, through building a renowned and respected public image.

Purchased goodwill

When one company purchases another company and pays an amount over and above the fair value of the net identifiable assets of the acquired business, then that excess amount is treated as goodwill.

IFRS 3 (which deals with business combinations) regulates the treatment of purchased goodwill. Initially, purchased goodwill is measured at the consideration paid at acquisition less the fair value of the net assets of the acquired entity:

Goodwill = Consideration paid – Net assets value of entity

For example, Y Company acquires Z Company for an amount of £2.95 million. Z Company had a net assets value (total assets less liabilities) of £2.3 million at the date of acquisition. Goodwill is therefore calculated as follows: £2.95 - £2.3 = £0.65 million

There might be times that **negative goodwill** arises on a business transaction. This will be when the contribution paid is less than the fair value of the net tangible assets. If so, then negative goodwill should be recognised in the statement of comprehensive income.

Internally generated goodwill

An internally generated goodwill is when an entity **incurs expenses** in the hopes of **increasing the possibility** of **future economic benefit**.

A good example of an internally generated goodwill is when money is spent on developing customer relationships. If an entity has better customer relationships, this will obviously lead to better sales performance and deeper customer loyalty. Furthermore, it will raise the market value of such an entity.

However, because it is difficult to quantify, **internally generated goodwill is never considered as an intangible asset**. Any expenditure incurred is directly expensed.

This rule does not only apply to goodwill, but also includes other internally generated items like brands, mastheads, publishing titles, customer lists, etc.

Research and development

It has been briefly mentioned that internally generated intangibles have additional recognition criteria that they have to fulfil. One of the most common aspects of internally generated intangibles is a **research and development phase** for a product. This is the stage at which a company is working on making an idea for a product a reality.

It is important that research costs can be identified separately from development costs, as these costs are recorded differently in the financial statements.

Research phase – Research costs are **expensed when incurred**. This is because the likelihood of future economic benefit is **uncertain** during the research phase, and so the costs cannot really be classified as an asset.

However, there will be times that research and development costs cannot be properly differentiated. In this case, the **whole amount** must then be expensed.

Development phase – During the development phase, it is possible for an entity to determine that the intangible asset (being developed) will generate future economic benefit for the business. If it is concluded as such, the **development costs** for the intangible asset **should be capitalised**.

According to IAS 38, an intangible asset should be recognised if an entity demonstrates all of the following:

- The technical feasibility of completing the intangible asset so that it can be used or sold

- The intention to complete the asset to use it or sell it

- The ability to use or sell the asset

- That the asset will in fact generate probable future economic benefit

- That it has the technical, financial and other resources to complete the project to make and use or sell the asset

- That it can measure the development cost of the asset reliably

Example

Let us take as an example a software developing company, Q Company. Q Company incurred various expenses to further develop its flagship software, QuCee. Differentiate research and development costs from the list of actions below:

Actions	Research or Development	Comment
Leased computer software used in R&D	Research	R&D costs cannot be properly separated
Correction of errors	Research	No certainty shown that it contributes to future economic benefit
Cost of software upgrade resulting in additional functionality	Development	Added value to the asset can be established because of additional functionality
Salaries of employees working directly on the projects (coding, software)	Development	At this stage (coding and setting-up), the decision to develop the software has already been made. There is a fair assumption that future economic benefit can be gained when the asset is complete.
Purging and cleaning existing data	Research	No change to the existing asset. No sign that future economic benefit will be generated

In-process research and development – A research and development project acquired during a merger or acquisition is recognised as an **asset at cost**, even if project is still in the research phase. Subsequently though, any additions to the project will be subject to the main recognition criteria of separating research and development costs.

3. Measurement

So, as we have seen, intangible assets can be tricky to quantify, and we need to make sure we are consistent in our approach to this. We are now going to look at the two main ways of measuring intangible assets: **the cost model** and **the revaluation model**.

When it comes to measurement, most intangible assets are initially measured at cost. For subsequent measurement after acquisition, the entity may use either the cost model or the revaluation model. However, once a measurement policy is chosen, it must be applied to all intangible assets in the same class.

Cost model

IAS 38 describes the **cost model** as intangible assets being **carried at cost less accumulated amortisation and impairment losses**.

Even though a re-valued amount for an intangible asset exists, if the company has already chosen to use the cost model, then the intangible asset will be **valued at historical cost**.

We will take a simple example of a franchise purchased at the original cost of £230,000 a number of years ago. The franchise is now worth £320,000. If the entity is using the **cost model** as its accounting policy, then the measurement of cost for this franchise will remain at £230,000 in the statement of financial position.

Revaluation model

IAS 38 describes the revaluation model as **intangible assets being carried at re-valued amounts** less any subsequent amortisation and impairment losses.

The re-valued amounts must be based on fair market value and must be determined by an active market. It is very rare to find active markets for intangible assets though. If no active market is found for the intangible asset, then only the cost model can be used.

Assuming that an active market can be found for the intangible asset and that the revaluation method is used, then the same logic as the rules for revaluing property, plant and equipment are followed.

Let us take our previous example of a franchise purchased at the original cost of £230,000 years ago. The franchise is now worth £320,000. If the company chooses the revaluation model as its accounting policy, then the additional increase of £90,000 would need to be recorded.

As in this case, if the re-valued amount is higher than the original cost, then the added amount is recognised in other comprehensive income as "**revaluation surplus**".

With our example, the entries will be as follows:

Debit	Intangible asset	£90,000	
Credit	Revaluation surplus		£90,000

However, if the value decreases, the difference will only be recorded in other comprehensive income provided there is a balance in the revaluation reserve account to cover it. If there is insufficient balance in the revaluation reserve account, then the difference will offset the account balance first, and the rest is then expensed in the profit and loss statement.

4. Accounting for amortisation

Useful life

As mentioned before, the two kinds of intangibles are **definite** and **indefinite** tangible assets.

A definite intangible asset, with its limited lifespan, should be amortised over its useful life. On the other hand, an indefinite intangible asset, with its infinite nature, should not be amortised at all.

The only time there is a change is if the useful life status of the intangible asset changes (mainly shifting from indefinite to definite). Subsequent amortisation should then be reviewed and undertaken.

A simple decision mapping exercise should assist when determining the useful life of an intangible asset:

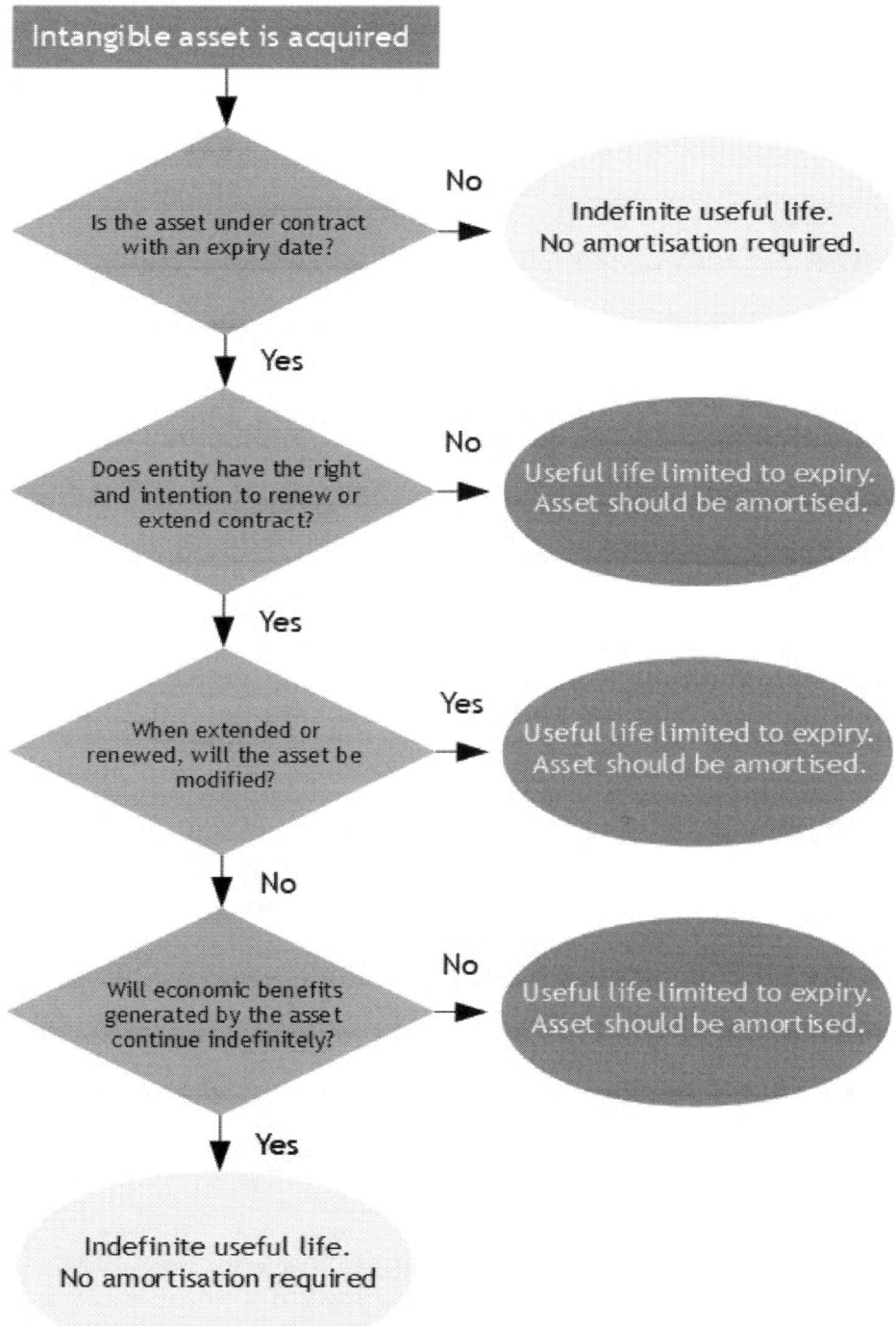

Amortisation

In some countries, amortisation is used interchangeably with depreciation. There is a slight difference between the two terms. **Amortisation is the systematic reduction of the value of an intangible asset over its useful life**. As opposed to depreciation which deals with tangible assets.

Amortisation should only start from the date that the intangible asset is available and ready for use. Amortisation should end as soon as the intangible asset is no longer in the control of the entity (when it is sold or disposed of).

The systematic way that an intangible asset is amortised should reflect the pattern in which the future economic benefits from that asset will be consumed or used.

The **straight-line amortisation** method should be chosen when the **consumption pattern** of an intangible asset **cannot be determined**.

This method involves using the capitalised cost of the intangible asset and reducing it evenly over its useful life. Most intangibles are amortised using the straight-line method.

Take Company J for example. Company J acquired a patent for £16,000, which allows the company to manufacture and sell a new technology for 20 years. The following calculations are raised:

$$\text{Amortisation} = \frac{\text{Cost of patent}}{\text{Useful life}}$$

$$= \frac{£16,000}{20 \text{ years}}$$

$$= £800$$

The amortisation of the patent annually is £800 for 20 years.

CIMA BA3 Study Text

Chapter 11

Dealing With Errors

1. Errors

In 2014, the Bank of America found that an error had crept into their accounts. That error had been there since 2009. The error totalled $4bn! Yes $4bn, and it hadn't been identified for all those years either by the company or by it's auditors, PwC. It related to a miscalculation of losses from the acquisition of investment bank Merrill Lynch.

Errors can be easy to make. Most are not as large as with the Bank of America, but all are important to identify and correct if it's easy to do.

Typical accounting errors

The following is a table of the main errors encountered when bookkeeping. Some of them are similar, but it is important to remember what each error refers to, and why they are different types of error.

Error	Explanation
Errors of omission	This occurs when **a transaction has been completely left out** or 'omitted' from both sides of the account.
Errors of commission	This happens when **one side of the transaction is debited or credited to the wrong account**. For instance, if money from a customer is credited to the payables and not the receivables account.
Errors of principle	This is similar to an error of commission, but with an important distinction. Rather than a transaction being posted to the wrong account, it is **posted to the wrong type of account**. For instance, if money from a customer is credited to the asset account and not the receivables account.
Errors of original entry	This occurs when the **correct accounts are debited and credited, but the values are both incorrect**. For instance, instead of debiting a wages account with £1,000 from the bank account, the wages account is debited with £10,000 from the bank account. An extra zero can make a big difference!
Reversal of entries	This error concerns **mixing up debits and credits**. For instance, if money from a customer is credited to the bank account and debited to receivables.

Error	Explanation
Compensation of errors	This error happens when **two separate mistakes are made that happen to cancel each other out.** So, for instance, wages debited with £100 instead of £1,000, but sales credited with £1,500 instead of £2,400. The problem here is that the error might not get spotted or might be hard to identify as the wages account looks like it is correct.
Duplication of entries	And finally, this error occurs when the same transaction is recorded twice.

2. Preventing errors

There are several measures a company can take in preventing errors from occurring.

Authorisation procedures

This measure simply means to make sure all actions are authorised by someone at the appropriate level.

For example, if a company is going to invest a large amount of money in purchasing a new non-current asset – such as a new office, or machinery – obviously these transactions will need authorisation from management to go ahead with the purchase.

In fact, **almost all activity will need some level of authorisation.** This can often appear to be time consuming and sometimes unnecessary, but it is very important in ensuring that mistakes are not made.

Documentation

Documentation serves as evidence of transactions. If you have ever wanted to return an unwanted item to a shop, you will know that you need a receipt. This is because the receipt is evidence of the transaction, and without it a business is susceptible to fraud.

Documentation within a business also helps to provide what is called an **audit trail**, which is a series of documents (invoices, receipts, purchases, etc.) that can be traced to a source, so that every penny is accounted for.

For example, if a company purchases goods that they will eventually sell on to customers, a series of steps will make up this process:

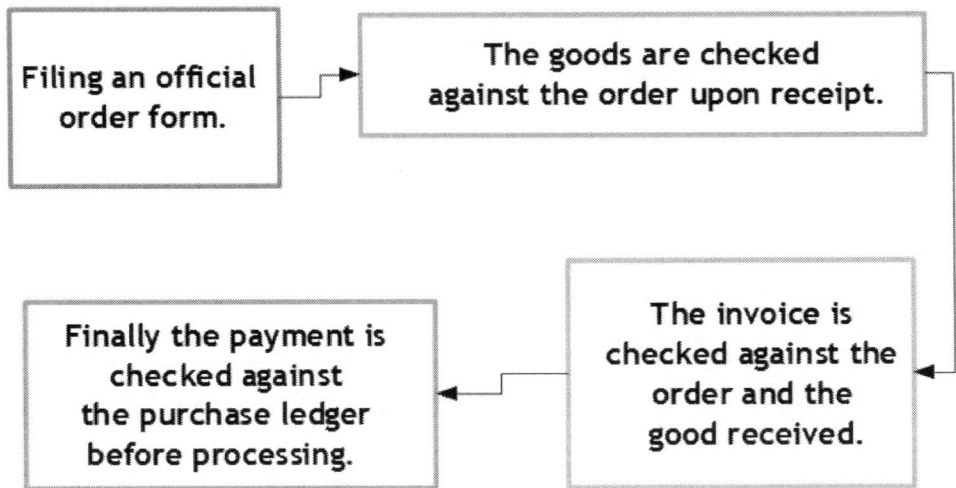

Organisation of staff

It is very important for a company to organise their staff appropriately so that mistakes are not made. Initially, a company needs to consider: who they recruit, whether the staff member has sufficient training, and what level of supervision they need.

Specifically for accounting, **no single person should be in control of one whole area of the ledger.** This is far too risky, since mistakes are more likely to be missed and fraud is harder to spot.

Therefore, we have what we call the **segregation of duties** which means that certain steps within a process are shared out accordingly. So, for example, one large sale may involve producing sales invoices, credit notes, banking receipts, etc. If a company really wants to reduce the risk of error, then processing of that sale would be shared across multiple staff members.

Safeguarding assets

A company should control their assets. **This includes maintenance, keeping the assets insured, making sure they are utilised, appropriately valued and recorded.**

3. Detecting errors

It should be assumed that, even with excellent systems in place to prevent errors, they still may occur. Therefore, we need ways to find them and correct them as quickly as possible.

Spot check

A spot check is essentially a random check made by a company to make sure procedures are being followed. These are particularly useful in detecting fraud within a company.

Comparison with external evidence

This one is quite self explanatory. **It simply involves comparing your books against external evidence from outside the company.** This could be obtaining a bank statement for the period in question, or equally, obtaining a statement from a customer/supplier from the relevant period.

Reconciliations

Let's say you suspect an error has been made somewhere in the system. One thing you can do is to **take your record and compare it with another record or statement with the intention of identifying the mistake and correcting it.**

There are a few different ways to do this:

- **Produce a trial balance** - and make sure it balances!

- **Reconcile accounts** - with external records from banks or suppliers

- **Control accounts** – e.g. comparing the sales ledger against the sales ledger control account (otherwise known as the receivables account) in the nominal ledger

More on reconciliations later in the chapter.

4. The correction of errors and suspense accounts

So, what happens if the trial balance doesn't balance and we cannot seem to find the error very quickly?

Well, this is what **suspense accounts** are for. **A suspense account is a temporary account used to offset any unbalanced accounts**, thus allowing us to prepare a financial statement subject to the correction of errors. We may need to do this, for example, if the

financial statements are due in a month but there are not the time or resources to correct all errors in time.

Alternatively we may simply **add all errors to the suspense account so they can all be dealt with at once at a later point.**

The balance of the suspense account is treated as an expense if it is a debit, and as a liability if it is a credit. This is because it is essentially an account that makes up for the difference in an unbalanced trial balance (or should that be trial unbalance?)

When the **errors are found**, often at a later date, they should be **corrected with an explanation**, initially in the journal, and then in the ledger accounts.

Example

Here we will look at how to clear the suspense account once the errors have been found and corrected in the accounts.

At the end of the period, a trial balance is written up in which the debit balance is £133 less than the credit balance. A suspense account is set up to balance the difference with the intention of fully correcting the error(s) in the next reporting period.

The following errors are later found:

1. A cheque to supplier W. White of £150 was recorded in the cash book, but not in the W. White sales ledger account, nor in the control account.

2. The expenses account was found to be £50 under cast.

3. A cheque from P. Griffin of £67 was recorded in the cash book, but not in the P. Griffin sales ledger account, nor the control account (receivables).

What we need to do first then is to record and correct the errors in the journal:

Journal	Dr(£)	Cr(£)
Payables (Purchase ledger control account)	150	
Suspense		150
(Correction of error: only the cash entry was posted)		
Expenses	50	
Suspense		50
(Correction of error: expenses under cast by £50)		
Suspense	67	
Receivables (Sales ledger control account)		67
(Correction of error: only the cash entry was posted)		

So, as you can see, we are essentially balancing the suspense account with each error that we have found. In the end, the total debit balance of the suspense account is removed by charging it to the places it should have been charged to in the first place.

Next, we balance the suspense account:

Suspense			
	£		£
Balance (from error in TB)	133	Payables	150
Receivables	67	Expenses	50
	200		200

So here, the suspense account had a debit balance caused by the 'extra' £133 found in the trial balance. Then we just apply the credit or debit as shown in the journal entries. This leads to the suspense account being balanced and all errors being corrected.

At this stage, we could then produce a corrected trial balance, simply by making the appropriate amendments from the original.

5. Reconciliation statements

Even the best of us will lose track of exactly where we are with our personal finances. Now, this could be for a number of reasons; perhaps you have your dates mixed up for a payment, and you've ended up with more than you expected. Or, perhaps you have less than you thought because you forgot about the time you decided to order a takeaway when you couldn't face doing any cooking after a long day of accounting! Usually this won't matter too much. You just notice the amount of money you have is slightly different from what you expected and move on with your life.

However, as we've already seen earlier in the chapter, when this happens in business, an entity will refer to what is called a reconciliation statement. The purpose of this is to **check the internal records against an external source, either to locate errors, or at least explain differences.** This is because having accurate financial reports is much more important for a business than an individual.

Bank reconciliation statement

A bank reconciliation is a process of comparing the company records against bank records in order to locate differences. Often, there will be timing issues with a bank (for processing payments etc.) and so we need to be aware of this.

astranti
financial training

Example

The following documents are used for reconciliation:

Cash book

		£				£
01st	Balance	1,200	18th	DOA		290
13th	TX	448	28th	RIP		144
13th	GI	372	30th	DD		218
				Balance c/d		1,368
		2,020				2,020
	Balance b/d	1,368				

Bank statement

		Out (£)	In (£)	Balance(£)
01st	Balance			1,270
03rd	PL	70		1,200
13th	TX		448	1,648
23rd	DOA	290		1,358
31st	Standing order	60		1,298

So, we can see that there are some differences here. Let's start with the opening balance which has a £70 difference on it. The PL entry in the bank statement, given the date, will most likely have been recorded in the cash book for the previous period. This is also why the balance in each document is different. Though our cash book had processed the PL payment, our bank statement showed it in a later period.

The RIP and DD transactions have not been recorded in the bank statement, but if we look at the date we can assume that they have not yet been processed. Perhaps they were for a cheque that has yet to clear through the bank statement at month end.

The receipt from GI appears not to have gone through the bank statement. That will need to be investigated. Perhaps a cheque has bounced, or not arrived at the bank.

So, the only real update we need to make is the standing order payment of £60. This looks to have been missed, perhaps because it is processed on the last day of the month.

So, let's update the cash book:

Cash book						
		Bank (£)				Bank (£)
01st	Balance b/f	1,200	18th	DOA		290
13th	TX	448	28th	RIP		144
13th	GI	372	30th	DD		218
			31st	Standing order		60
				Balance c/d		1,308
		2,020				2,020
	Balance b/d	1,308				

Now we need to draw up a bank reconciliation statement to actually see what is going on a little more clearly:

	(£)
Balance as per bank statement	1,298
Add: receipts not lodged (GI)	372
Less: unpresented cheques (RIP + DD)	(362)
	1,308

The discrepancy between the balance in our cash book and the bank statement has thus been reconciled, since we have accounted for the difference. Further work will need to go into investigating the GI difference as this is the only unusual item.

Reconciliation of suppliers' statements

Most companies will provide a statement for their customers. These will include things such as orders placed, returns, payments received and the outstanding balance due.

The concept of reconciliation is exactly the same here as for the bank records. The only difference may be that a supplier uses a bit more terminology than a bank. Here is a quick list of abbreviations that tend to be used in supplier statements:

- **BCE** – balance.

- **CHQ** – cheque.

- **GDS** – goods.

- **ALLCE** – allowance.

- **DISC** – discount.

- **ADJ** – adjustment.

These abbreviations will denote how particular sums of money are calculated. As you can see, most of them are pretty easy to figure out anyway!

Petty cash reconciliation

The petty cash book is used to record small cash transactions. It works on an imprest system, which means a 'float' is set for petty cash and is topped up from the bank account periodically.

For example, you might have a petty cash float of £50. That means there is physically £50 in notes or coins in a petty cash box. If a member of staff needs to buy some ink for a printer, for example, costing £20, they would take £20 from the petty cash box and purchase the ink. Then, they put the receipt for the ink in the petty cash box, along with the remaining £30. The receipt shows a payment worth £20, and there is £30 left in cash, so the total in the box is £50.

Eventually, the receipt will be filed and the petty cash box will be topped up to £50 again by withdrawing £20 from the bank account and putting it in the box.

Using this system, it is possible to reconcile the 'float' with the balance of cash in the box and receipts for purchases made.

Example

Let's say we have a petty cash system that is restored to £50 at the end of each month, and we have the following information regarding petty cash payments during March:

01st	Postage stamps	£1.00
03rd	Train ticket	£4.65
04th	Taxi fare	£5.00
08th	Stationary	£3.20
12th	Coffee	£2.20
14th	Lunch for visitors	£15.26
20th	Envelopes	£1.50
24th	Office plant	£4.50

Totalling up all of the purchases above gives us £37.31, which means a top up of £37.31 will be needed in the petty cash book. However, there is only £11 in cash in the petty cash box, which would only take us up to £48.31.

A member of staff remembers that they purchased some cleaning materials but forgot to keep the receipt. This explains the missing figure, and so we can assume that those cleaning materials cost £1.69 (£50 - £48.31).

Therefore, the top up required will be £37.31 + £1.69 = £39, and we also have a full account of the purchases made during the month. These expenses will be recorded in the petty cash book and then debited to the various relevant accounts in the nominal ledger.

Control accounts

You may remember from the bookkeeping process that accounting entries are made to both a book of prime entry, such as a sales daybook, and a control account (also known as a memorandum ledger).

For example, a sale is made to the sales day book, and to the sales ledger. The sales ledger contains amounts owed by each customer on a customer by customer basis.

The books of prime entry are totalled and entered into the nominal ledger.

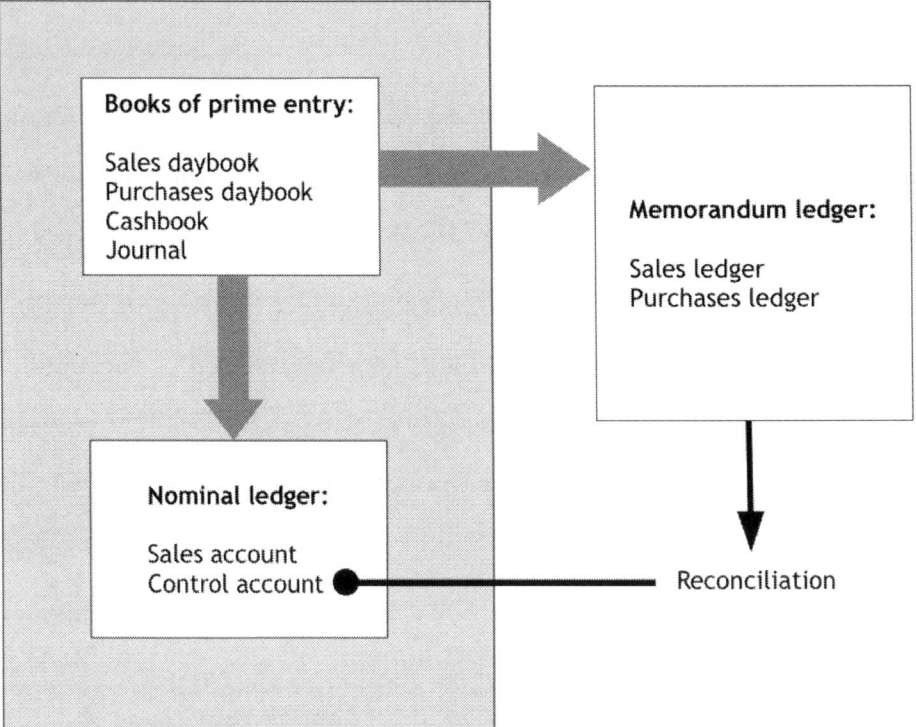

As we have the same records in two different internal systems this allows us to compared them to ensure the totals are the same. If they are not then there is an error in one of them.

So, it's quite clear that the memorandum ledgers are important, but it is essential to keep them outside of the double-entry system.

Advantages of control accounts

There are multiple reasons why control accounts are used in accounting.

Here are just a few:

- **For different information** – e.g. the sales ledger control account holds information on a customer by customer basis

- **They help to check accuracy in bookkeeping** – as we mentioned, having a control means you can compare figures to make sure mistakes aren't being made, and if they are, where to find them

- **They help with the segregation of duties** – With control accounts, no one person should be responsible for an entire area of the ledger (i.e. the control serves as a check)

- **Increase speed of bookkeeping** – through identifying errors quickly (which hopefully saves time compared to making all entries in two different systems!)

6. Contra entries

Let's say that you're a business that buys from and sells goods to another business. Suppose you are a baker, and you buy your meat from a butcher, but he also buys his bread from you. **Here we have a scenario where money is going to and coming from one place, and we can offset these cost to avoid unnecessary transactions. The record we make of this offset is called a contra entry.**

So, if you bought some meat for £100 and sold the butcher bread for £50, this would 'contra' so that you just paid £50 for the meat and the butcher pays nothing.

This is how the baker's sales and purchase ledgers would look:

Sales Ledger				
		Butcher		
Bread	100	Purchase led. (contra)	50
		Balance b/d	50
	100		100

Purchase ledger				
		Butcher		
Sales ledger (contra)	50	Meat	50
	50		50

We can see that the final position is that nothing is owed on the purchase ledger, and a balance of £50 is left owed from the butcher on the sales ledger.

Of course, matching entries would also be required in the nominal ledger accounts too – otherwise the nominal ledger and the control accounts wouldn't balance.

CIMA BA3 Study Text

Chapter 12

The Manufacturing Account

1. Introduction

Manufacturing businesses are a bit different to other businesses and therefore, their accounts are a bit different too. Don't panic, it's not too complicated, as soon as you think about how manufacturing businesses are different from others, it's much easier to follow and remember the differences in their accounts.

Let's look at a company that mass produces cakes. They buy flour, eggs, milk sugar, etc., and then mix it all together to make a lot of cakes. They then sell those cakes to supermarkets. Super simple stuff, right?

Yes, it is simple, but how do you show that in your accounts? The inventory has changed from raw materials (eggs, flour) to finished goods (cakes) without losing or gaining anything; it's just been converted.

Well, hang on a minute, we've forgot something quite important. What about the costs of production? Labour, electricity, rent and other bills. All of these can contribute to the cost of inventory. In a manufacturing company, we need to make sure we are showing these costs in the statements too.

So, let's take a look to see how manufacturing accounts are recorded.

Statement of financial position

Generally speaking, there aren't a huge amount of differences in the financial statements when it comes to manufacturing businesses. However, since manufacturers deal in raw materials and finished goods, the organisation of their inventories are slightly different. **We break down their inventories in the statement of financial position as follows:**

- **Bought-in-goods:** These are finished goods that the company have purchased. In our example above, this could be packaging that has been bought from packaging producers. The company doesn't make the packaging themselves; they just buy it in from someone else.

- **Finished goods:** These are finished goods that the company have produced themselves. This would be the finished cakes, in our example.

- **Work-in-progress:** These are raw materials that have begun to be processed but are incomplete. So this could be the sponge of the cake that needs to be cut up into individual cakes or have icing put on.

- **Raw materials:** These are the unprocessed materials that are not yet in production. In our example above, this included flour, eggs, sugar and milk, etc.

Income statement

Similarly, the income statement remains the same for the most part. **One key difference is that it will show 'the cost of finished goods manufactured' rather than 'cost of goods sold'.**

This does lead to a difference in calculation in the income statement. Establishing the cost of manufactured goods is a slightly more involved task than we have previously come across. We'll see how this is done in a moment.

The purpose of the manufacturing account

The income statement is used to bring together revenue earned and expenditure incurred by a business during a period of their trading. This ultimately generates a gross and net profit by subtracting all costs from all income.

The manufacturing account is a **sub-section of the income statement** (like the trading account) in which we calculate the **total made in manufacturing, less the costs incurred in manufacturing**.

2. Costs to include in the manufacturing account

When we are calculating the cost of manufacturing, there are a number of extra things we have to take into account in preparing the statement.

Raw materials

The direct costs are the raw materials, as these are what are purchased to ultimately produce a finished product. We can calculate the cost of raw materials in the same way that we calculate inventories in the income statement.

So, for our cake company, we have the following information:

	£
Opening inventory of raw materials	1,100
Add: Purchases of raw materials	24,250
Less: Closing inventories of raw materials	(1,250)
Cost of raw materials	24,100

As you should notice, this is the same principle used when calculating cost of sales in a normal income statements. Simple!

Other direct costs

Other direct costs include such things as the **cost of production** (i.e. the cost of direct labour/manpower in producing the finished good), and the expenses incurred on such things as **equipment hire for specialist production, the cost of power for machinery, and any royalties payable on the production of particular products.**

At our cake company, wages paid directly to employees who work in production cost £15,500, and the direct cost in running the factory in order to make the cakes is £8,500. These would be included as other direct costs, alongside the cost of raw materials.

Prime cost

So, the prime cost is simply **the total of all of the direct costs**. Let's see what our prime cost at the cake company is so far:

	£
Opening inventory of raw materials	1,100
Add: Purchases of raw materials	24,250
Less: Closing inventories of raw materials	(1,250)
Cost of raw materials	24,100
Direct manufacturing wages	15,500
Direct factory expenses	8,500
Prime cost	**48,100**

Indirect cost

In this section, we include **all other production costs that are not covered in the direct costs** (often referred to as **factory or production overheads**). This will include things such as:

- Factory rent

- Heat, light, and insurance

- Wages/salaries for factory supervisors/engineers

- Depreciation of non-current assets used in manufacturing

All of these things are obviously costs that enable the company to produce cakes, but they aren't directly related to the production process. This is why they are 'indirect', but they are still important.

At the cake company, the factory rent is £4,000, heating and lighting costs £1,200 and the wages for the factory supervisor come to £25,000.

Factory costs incurred

The factory costs incurred is **the total of the indirect costs plus the prime cost.** So, basically, another sub-total! Let's add the indirect costs to the prime cost to find the factory costs incurred at the cake company:

		£
Opening inventories of raw materials		1,100
Purchases of raw materials		24,250
Closing inventories of raw materials		(1,250)
Raw materials consumed		24,100
Direct manufacturing wages		15,500
Direct factory expenses		8,500
Prime cost		48,100
Production overhead		
Factory supervisors wages	25,000	
Heating and lighting	1,200	
Factory rent	4,000	
		30,200
Factory costs incurred		**78,300**

Work in progress

Next we need to include the work-in-progress cost (that's the cost of things such as the sponge waiting to be cut into cakes, or the icing yet to be applied). To do this, we enter the opening work-in-progress figure, and deduct the closing work-in-progress-figure, just like we would with any inventory.

So in at the cake company, we have an opening work-in-progress of £2,000 which includes the sponges and icing and we have a closing work-in-progress of £750.

Factory cost of goods completed

And finally, just like the gross profit in the trading account, and net profit in the income statement, **the factory cost of goods completed is the final cost we calculate in the manufacturing account.**

So, putting together everything we have so far, we get:

		£
Opening inventories of raw materials		1,100
Purchases of raw materials		24,250
Closing inventories of raw materials		(1,250)
Raw materials consumed		24,100
Direct manufacturing wages		15,500
Direct factory expenses		8,500
Prime cost		48,100
Production overhead		
Factory supervisors wages	25,000	
Heating and lighting	1,200	
Factory rent	4,000	
		30,200
Factory costs incurred		78,300
Opening work-in-progress	2,000	
Closing work-in-progress	(750)	
		1,250
Factory cost of goods completed		79,550

And that's the manufacturing account!

In finding the total cost of manufacturing, the manufacturing account can be said to be made up of 3 elements:

- **The cost directly attributed to goods produced** (raw material, wages, etc.)

- **The indirect costs** (rent, bills, factory staff, etc.)

- **The adjustment of opening and closing work-in-progress**

3. The layout of the manufacturing account

Okay, so what we need to do now is look at **how the manufacturing account fits within the income statement**. We've already got our manufacturing account, so what we do now is just include it within the income statement calculation.

Income Statement

So, as usual, the income statement will start with sales and then subtract the cost of goods sold. **Since the manufacturing account makes up part of the cost of sales, we need to include it here**.

Now, if you've been really observant you may have noticed that in our example to date we've considered inventory of raw materials, and work-in-progress, not finished goods e.g. those cakes that were finished but not sold at the year end. We include that here.

	£	£
Sales		95,000
Opening inventories of finished goods	5,800	
Spending on goods produced (Manufacturing account)	X	
Closing inventories of finished goods	(2,500)	
Costs of goods sold		X

The total amount spent on producing finished goods is simply the total previously obtained in the manufacturing account and so we **include the manufacturing account between opening and closing inventories of finished goods**.

So, let's do that in full with our example. We will start with sales, including opening finished goods, and then we'll add the manufacturing account. Beneath that we can include closing inventory to find gross profit.

Let's take a look.

	£	£	£	£
Sales				95,000
Opening inventories of finished goods			5,800	
Opening inventories of raw materials		1,100		
Purchases of raw materials		24,250		
Closing inventories of raw materials		(1,250)		
Raw materials consumed		24,100		
Direct manufacturing wages		15,500		
Direct factory expenses		8,500		
Prime cost		48,100		
Production overhead				
Factory supervisors wages	25,000			
Heating and lighting	1,200			
Factory rent	4,000			
		30,200		
Factory costs incurred		78,300		
Opening work-in-progress	2,000			
Closing work-in-progress	(750)			
		1,250		
Factory cost of goods completed			79,550	
			85,350	
Closing inventories of finished goods			(2,500)	
Cost of goods sold				(82 850)
Gross profit				12,150

The highlighted section above demonstrates the manufacturing account inserted into the income statement to show the spending on goods produced.

As you can see, much like previous income statements, it is simply a methodical way of calculating costs and comparing them against revenue.

4. The accounting system

Finally, let's think about how the accounting system for manufacturing accounts works. Luckily there is not really anything new to learn.

When it comes to accounting for a manufacturing account, all we do is create accounts in the nominal ledger such as:

- Direct manufacturing wages

- Direct factory expenses

- Inventories of raw materials

- Inventories of work-in-progress

- Inventories of finished goods

And we treat them in exactly the same way as all other ledgers, making sure we adhere to the double-entry convention. So, in the ledger, we will have a 'manufacturing account' which is debited and credited accordingly.

Example

For example, 'direct manufacturing wages ' costs would be debited to the direct manufacturing wages account during the year as paid. Direct factory labour represents an increase in expenses, so using DEADCLIC, we know it should be a debit – **DE**ad clic.

Then, at the end of the period the balance is transferred to the manufacturing account (as part of the income statement) by crediting the direct factory labour account and debiting the manufacturing account so that the labour account is closed to zero.

	Direct manufacturing wages		
Bank	£15,500	Manufacturing account	£15,500
	£15,500		£15,500

	Manufacturing account	
Direct factory labour	£15,500	

Finally, at the end of the year, the balance of the manufacturing account is transferred to the statement of profit or loss, and the total of that then shown in the income statement.

CIMA BA3 Study Text

Chapter 13

Incomplete Records

1. Missing figures

Kim owns a small business selling bespoke desk lamps online. Sometimes Kim makes mistakes and finds that she has lost the figures for certain transactions.

Kim needs to resolve the issues she had with her finances. Luckily for Kim there is a way **of figuring out the value of missing figures – called incomplete records.**

Sales figures

Let's say that a business has misplaced their opening receivables figures, they have not recorded their cash sales, and they have also overlooked customer discounts.

Even if we have a lot of missing information from the accounting books, there are ways **we can get some missing information through other means:**

- We will probably know the opening receivables from the **previous statement of financial position**.

- We will also probably know the closing receivables (customers who owe us money), as this is almost always recorded in some form, perhaps in a **sales ledger.**

- **Bank statements** will indicate the amount received from customers, so we have a record of sales there.

- We may also have **records of cash sales**, for instance through till receipts.

In this case, we can draw up the equivalent of a receivables account (otherwise known as the sales ledger control account), insert all known information about the sales, and derive the missing information as a balancing figure.

To see how this works let's say we have the following information about the transactions of Kim's business gleaned from various sources:

As of the 1st of January:

- They had receivables (balance b/f) of **£4,050,**

- Received **£21,000** in cheques from customers after **£300** of discounts,

- Written off bad debt of **£750**, and

- Had closing receivables of **£3,675**

Putting this into a 'control' account gives us:

	Receivables (SLCA)				
20X1		£	20X1		£
1st Jan	Balance b/f	4,050	In year	Bank	21,000
In year	Sales	?	In year	Cash discount	300
			In year	Bad debts	750
			31st Dec	Balance c/d	3,675
		25,725			25,725

So, we find the missing sales figure to be (£25,725 - £4,050) **£21,675,** and so this is our estimate. We can estimate missing figures for purchases and expenses in exactly the same fashion, just making sure to debit and credit the right accounts with the right amounts.

Capital

Kim is missing her opening capital figure.

In this case she can usually use the accounting equation to calculate the missing figures:

Accounting equation: Assets = Liabilities + Capital

For example, if she knows that total assets at the start of the year came to £2,000 and total liabilities were £1,500, then she also knows that the opening capital must be £500 (assets – liabilities).

Drawings

Next let's imagine that Kim has recorded everything correctly, but has not recorded her drawings – the money she takes out of the business for her own use.

She can firstly work out her end of year capital using the accounting equation (assets – liabilities).

Then she can be aware that the **only reason why capital would change would be:**

- **New capital**

- **Net profit/loss**

- **Drawings**

The equation to work out capital would look like this:

Opening capital + new capital + profit – drawings = Closing capital

So, if the year end capital is £3,000, she added £1,000 of new capital during the year and had profits of £10,000 then we can substitute these figures into the equation.

£500 + £1,000 + £10,000 - Drawings = £3,000

£11,500 - Drawings = £3,000

Drawings = £8,500

2.   Cash and bank summaries

Usually, enquires about incomplete records start with a summary of cash and bank transactions (called a receipt and payment account). Let's see how we can use these to find missing information with an example.

Example

Bill Burr does not keep full accounting records. He can, however, provide us with the following information for the year ending 31st Dec 20X8:

	01st Jan	31st Dec
Inventories	£4,950	£5,270
Receivables	£750	£925
Payables for purchases	£1,200	£1,475
Accrued wages payable	£235	£300

In addition, by looking at all the available information he has, we are able to draw up the following cash and bank summary:

Cash	£	Bank	£
Opening balance	1,020	Opening balance	11,550
Receipts		Receipts	
Shop takings	9,775	Customer cheques	3,015
Cash withdrawn - bank	525	Shop takings paid in	6,500
	11,320		21,065
Payments		Payments	
Purchases	(720)	Purchases	(6,900)
Wages	(195)	Wages	(1,750)
Other expenses	(250)	Other expenses	(1,075)
Drawings	(1,525)	Purchase of van	(950)
Paid into bank	(6,500)	Cash withdrawn	(525)
Closing balance	2,130	Closing balance	9,865

Bill also believed that one customer owing £45 will not pay which had been written off during the year.

The van is to be depreciated at 20% per annum (straight-line, no residual value).

Now, using this information, we can prepare financial statements by working out missing figures and filling in the gaps. Let's go through the workings so that we can produce the income statement.

Workings

1. Sales

Firstly Bill needs to work out sales.

He can start with the receivables account here – as credit sales is one of the key items in that account which he should be able to work out.

Let's start by putting in the start and end year balances. Receivables is an asset and an asset balance will be a debit.

Receivables

	£		£
Balance b/f	750		
Credit sales	?		
		Balance c/d	925
	13,145		13,145

Bill has written off a £45 debt, so that must be a credit to receivables to counteract the debit balance we'd normally expect on receivables.

Receivables

	£		£
Balance b/f	750	Bad debt	45
Credit sales	?		
		Balance c/d	925
	13,145		13,145

Looking at the bank account we also have cheques paid by customers, which we will assume relate to credit sales – that's £3,015.

Receivables

	£		£
Balance b/f	750	Bad debt	45
Credit sales (bal. fig.)	**3,235**	Bank	3,015
		Balance c/d	925
	3,985		3,985

Balancing this account leaves us with a **balancing figure on receivables of £3,235** which is the total credit sales.

To find total sales we also need to **add in the shop takings in cash of £9,775** to get **total sales of £13,010**.

2. Purchases

The purchases and expense accounts are typically dealt with on an individual basis when doing incomplete records questions.

You'll notice that the question gives us the payables related to purchases made in the business, so we can work out purchases separately from any other expenses.

We do a similar process here as above but this time to find the credit purchases:

Payables (Purchases only)			
	£		£
		Balance b/f	1,200
Bank	6,900	Credit purchases (bal. fig)	**7,175**
Balance c/d	1,475		
	8,375		8,375

We can then **add on the cash purchases of £720** to get a **total purchases figure of £7,895**.

3. Wages

Next we'll calculate the wages in a similar way.

We are given the starting and ending accrual for wages. Remember an accrual is an amount owed (in this case wages owed to staff), and so it is a credit balance. Let's add these into a wages account.

Wages account			
	£		£
		Balance b/f	235
Balance c/d	300		

We've paid some wages from the bank and some in cash, so let's add both of those in. The balancing item is then the wages for the year.

Wages account			
	£		£
Cash	195	Balance b/f	235
Bank	1,750	Wages (bal. fig)	**2,010**
Balance c/d	300		
	2,245		2,245

4. Other expenses

As there are no brought forward or carried forward balances for other expenses, we can just assume that the amounts paid (bank + cash) are the expenses incurred. This totals £1,325 (£1,075 + £250).

5. Van

The purchase of the van is not an expense as it is the purchase of an asset. However, this will be depreciated each year and so in the income statement a depreciation charge will need to be made:

Cost of van: £950, depreciation @ 20% = £190 depreciation charge

Income Statement

Now that we have done our workings, we can go ahead and draw up our income statement.

Income statement for the period ending 31st December 20X8

	£	£
Sales (W1)		13,010
Opening inventories	4,950	
Purchases (W2)	7,895	
	12,845	
Less: closing inventories	(5,270)	
Cost of goods sold		(7,575)
Gross profit		5,435
Wages (W3)	2,010	
Other expenses	1,325	
Bad debts	45	
Depreciation	190	
		(3,570)
Net profit		**1,865**

3. Gross profit mark-up and margin

Gross profit mark-up

If you sell goods worth £1,000 for £1,500 then that means you will have made a gross profit of £500. You can also say that the goods had a mark-up of 50%. This simply means that the selling price of the goods was increased by 50%:

£1,000 x 50% = £500

£1,000 + £500 = £1,500

A simpler way to calculate a mark-up is to multiply by 1.x, where x is the percentage shown as a decimal. So, in this case, we would do:

£1,000 x 1.50 = £1,500.

(A 12% mark-up would be 1.12, and a 13.456% mark-up would be 1.13456.)

Knowing this means that we can calculate either the sales figure or the cost of goods sold figure, as long as we know the mark-up. The important thing to remember for a mark-up is that **cost of goods sold always represent 100%**. In this case our cost of goods sold was £1,000, that's 100%. With the mark up added the sales price is £1,500 so 150%.

Finding cost of goods sold

So, if we had a different scenario where we know sales were £25,000 and the mark-up was 25%, that means the cost of goods sold were increased by 25% to get sales. We can then find the cost of goods sold by doing:

Cost of goods sold x 1.25 = £25,000

Re-arranging gives us:

$$\frac{£25,000}{1.25} = £20,000$$

So, knowing sales was £25,000 and that the mark-up was 25%, we could calculate that cost of goods sold was £20,000.

Finding sales

If we have cost of goods sold and the mark-up, then the job is a simpler one. If we have cost of goods sold of £3,000 and a mark-up of 10%, then we do:

£3,000 x 1.10 = £3,300

So the sales figure is £3,300.

Gross profit margin

The gross profit margin is where **the profit is based on the sales price** instead of the cost of goods sold. In this case, the **sales price represents 100%**.

Finding cost of goods sold

So, if we had sales of £12,000 and a margin of 15%, that means that 15% of the £12,000 is the profit, and the remaining amount (in this case 85%) is the cost of goods sold. Therefore, the calculation is:

£12,000 x 85% = £10,200 for cost of goods sold.

Finding sales

If we don't know sales, but know the cost of goods sold, the calculation is reversed. If our cost of goods sold is £15,000 and the margin is 25%, then we know that £15,000 is equal to 75% of whatever the sales figure is. To find sales (which is 100%, remember) then, we do:

$$\frac{£15,000}{75} \quad x \quad 100 = \quad £20,000$$

So, the sales figure in this case is £20,000.

A quicker way to do this is:

$$\frac{£15,000}{0.75} \quad = \quad £20,000$$

If you aren't comfortable doing it that way then there's nothing wrong with doing it the first way!

CIMA BA3 Study Text

Chapter 14

The Statement of Cash Flows

1.   The Statement of Cash Flows

If you take a look at your bank balance you will (hopefully) see a lump sum of cash. That's great, but where did it all come from? You probably have income from your wages, so that's some of it, but then maybe you also have interest to add on from the bank. Perhaps you also sold an old sofa on eBay and you received a payment from PayPal, which is in there somewhere, too.

How about your outgoings? Costs for rent, food, bills, taxes perhaps. They've all been taken out, but all you see now is the current balance. Wouldn't it be useful to have a statement that broke down the inward and outward flow of cash from your bank account? Something that would show you how you spent your money grouped into categories such as rent, food, eating out and so on. This might be particularly useful if you'd just gone into overdraft and weren't sure how that happened!

This is roughly the thinking behind our next financial statement, The Statement of Cash Flows. Companies produce them to help them understand how they spent their cash. **Some companies can be quite profitable, and yet have a negative cashflow for the period,** perhaps due to investment in new assets without sufficient new funding, or due to a significant purchases of new inventory that has yet to be sold and so are not recognised in the income statement.

The Statement of Cash Flows helps the readers of the accounts understand the cash position and helps them assess if there are any serious cashflow issues which have not been highlighted in the income statement or statement of financial position.

How it works

Cash flow statements are another **primary financial statement**, in addition to the statement of financial position and the statement of comprehensive income. Very simply, cash flow statements tell us **how much cash the company has at the end of the year, how much it had at the start of the year, and the change in cash from the start to the end of the year:**

Opening cash	xx	A
Closing cash	xx	B
Change in cash	xx	B - A

The change in cash is calculated by looking at what a business has paid in cash during a financial year (**cash outflows**) and what it has received in cash (**cash inflows**) during the same period.

The difference between the inflows and outflows will give us the overall change in cash flows for the year, e.g.:

Cash inflows	xx
Cash outflows	(xx)
Change in cash flows	xx

Obviously, if the cash outflows are greater than the inflows, then the company will have less cash at the end of the year than it started with. Is this a bad thing? Well, that depends, and is why the statement of cash flows is useful, because it shows why **a decrease in cash doesn't always represent a decrease in value**. A growing company, for instance, would expect to be investing cash inflows in new assets as a way to grow the business so the change in cash flows will be negative for a very good reason.

Cash only

The key to understanding this statement is to know that it deals only with cash. Therefore, it **will only include transactions that involved a payment or a receipt of money**. This is different to the statement of comprehensive income, which may include non-cash transactions, such as depreciation, accruals and prepayments. For this reason, **it is possible for a business to look profitable in its comprehensive income, and problematic in liquidity in its cash flow statement**, and vice versa.

The difference between profit and cash

We mentioned a moment ago that a decrease in cash doesn't always mean a decrease in overall value, but what did we mean by that? The key to understanding this lies in the **difference between cash and profit**.

Cash is money, but money isn't the only thing of value. Imagine you buy an old lamp at a charity shop for £20. However, it turns out that the lamp is an antique and is actually worth £1,000. What's going on with the cash flows here?

Well, initially, your cash balance decreased by £20 when you paid for the lamp, even though you actually acquired something worth £1,000. So, from a purely cash perspective, you are down £20. However, in terms of overall value (or profit) you have made £980 because of the true value of the lamp.

So this is the idea of the statement of cash flows: **it shows the change in cash balance only**. Once you can sell the lamp for £1,000, the cash flow statement will recognise a cash inflow of £1,000, a cash outflow of £20 and an overall cash increase of £980.

Hopefully this example made the concept clear, but there are actually **3 main reasons why it is important to make the distinction between cash and profit in accounting**:

- **Revenue is claimed when earned, not received** – Usually, revenue is recognised as soon as a transaction is identified according to the proper rules. However, this doesn't always mean that cash is received. For example, receivables represent cash owed by customers, which means that the company doesn't have that cash yet, even though the revenue will be recognised in the income statement.

- **The profit calculation includes non-cash transactions** - So, for example, the depreciation charge is subtracted from the gross profit during the net profit calculation, but it involves no movement of cash.

- **The cash balance can be affected by things that will not affect profit** – For instance, the purchasing of a non-current asset requires an outflow of cash for an investment in non-current assets. Overall, assets will increase, but this will not increase the profit for the period.

Format of the statement of cash flows

IAS 7 Statement of Cash Flows

IAS 7 – Statement of Cash Flows, requires a specific format for cash flow statements. This format splits the cash flows of a business into **three different activities**:

- **Operating activities** – cash flows related to operations, e.g. sales, costs, expenses

- **Investing activities** – cash related to investments, e.g. purchasing non-current assets, buying shares

- **Financing activities** – cash related to raising finance, e.g. bank loans, issuing shares

The cash flow statement ends with the **net increase or decrease in the cash and equivalents,** which is the difference between the cash and cash equivalents at the beginning, and at the end of the year.

Statement of Cash Flows		Company A (increase)	Company B (decrease)
		£	£
Operating activities	xx	540,000	28,000
Investing activities	xx	(46,000)	(125,000)
Financing activities	xx	5,000	70,000
Net change in cash flows	xx	499,000	(27,000)
Opening cash balance	xx	1,000,000	1,000,000
Closing cash balance	xx	£1,499,000	£973,000

So which of these two companies would you prefer to invest in? Almost certainly A. Much stronger operating activity cash flows suggest an inherently better business. Even then the cash flow position is not enough for a full picture – we'd need to see the income statement and financial position before we could really decide.

2. Cash flow from operating activities

Introduction

Cash flows from operating activities are generated from the on-going operational activities of the business. **Operating cash flows are the principal financing source** a business uses to maintain and develop its operational capability. They are mainly associated with the '**working capital**' accounts of a business, such as the **accounts receivable, accounts payable and inventory**.

Inflows and outflows

Inflows

The following are some examples of cash **inflows** (cash going in to the entity) from operating activities:

- Cash **receipts** from the **sale of goods** and services – e.g. The cash McDonald's receive when they sell a hamburger

- Cash **receipts** from **contracts held** for trading purposes – e.g. The cash received from an entity with whom you a have a contract to build a house

- **Refunds of income taxes** (unless they can be specifically identified with financing or investing) – e.g. The cash received from tax authorities for overpaying tax in a previous tax year

Cash outflows

The following are some examples of cash **outflows** (cash leaving the entity) from operating activities:

- **Payments to suppliers for goods and services** - e.g. Cash paid out to a farmer for milk from an ice cream manufacturer

- **Payments to employees** – e.g. Cash paid out in the form of wages/salaries

- **Payments** from **contracts held** for trading purposes – e.g. paying a contractor for their work

There are **two methods** that can be used to calculate cash flows from operating activities – the *direct* method and the *indirect* method.

The Direct Method

The direct method basically starts with cash collected during the year and subtracts cash paid to find the total cash from operations. The result is an accurate indication of precisely **what funds were collected in the form of cash or paid in the form of cash**. This means that the direct method is very useful for investors, but it's more complicated for accountants!

Fortunately, **the direct method is not required at BA3**, so you don't to know how to do it!

The Indirect Method

The second method of doing our cash flow statement is much easier. Phew! The information it provides isn't quite so useful to the user though, so there's a bit of give and take here. Having said that is it very common in practice (perhaps because us accountants like the easy way out!).

Under the indirect method, there are 3 main steps:

1. **Identify net profit** from the statement of comprehensive income

2. **Adjust the non-cash items** in the statement of comprehensive income – such as depreciation

3. **Calculate the changes in the working capital** items of the statement of financial position

This leaves us with something looking like this:

Profit before taxation	xx
Adjustments:	
Depreciation	xx
Gain on disposal of non-current asset	(xx)
Working capital changes:	
(Increase)/Decrease in trade receivables	xx
(Increase)/Decrease in inventories	(xx)
Increase/(Decrease) in trade payables	xx
Cash generated from operating activities	**xx**

The Indirect Method: Example

The easiest way to understand the indirect method is through an example, so let's start with the two statements that we need in order to produce the cash flow statement: the statement of financial position and the statement of comprehensive income:

Success Company	**31.12.X4**
Statement of Comprehensive Income	**$'000**
Sales	140
Cost of goods sold	(96)
Gross profit	**44**
Other income	10
Operating expenses	(22)
Loss on disposal of non-current assets	(1)
Depreciation	(17)
Interest expenses	(2)
Interest received	1
Profit before tax	**13**
Income tax	(3)
Net profit after tax	**10**

Success Company *Statement of Financial Position*	31.12.X4 $'000	31.12.X3 $'000
Non-current assets		
Tangible assets	85	70
Current assets		
Inventory	30	30
Trade receivables	60	20
Prepaid operating expenses	3	–
Cash in bank and hand	162	135
Total assets	**340**	**255**
Equity & Liabilities		
Issued share capital	70	60
Share premium account	30	20
Revaluation reserve	25	20
Accumulated profits	80	70
	205	**170**
Non-current liabilities		
Loans	87	58
	87	**58**
Current liabilities		
Trade payables	45	25
Accrued operating expenses	3	2
	48	**27**
Total Equity & Liabilities	**340**	**255**

Notes:

1. Success Company disposed of tangible assets in 20X4 with a net book value of $8,000.

Okay, so here are the steps for using the indirect method:

1. Identify net profit before tax from the statement of comprehensive income.

This is the starting figure and we can it take directly from the statement of comprehensive income. For Success Company, the figure to start with is $13,000.

2. Adjust the non-cash items in the statement of comprehensive income.

The statement of comprehensive income is prepared using the **accrual basis** of accounting. This means that the profit or loss before taxation is a result of both **cash items and non-cash items** in the year.

For instance, in the income statement, profit before tax will have had a number of expenses deduced or added, but not all of them represent a cash outflow:

Success Company	31.12.X4
Statement of Comprehensive Income	$'000
Sales	140
Cost of goods sold	(96)
Gross profit	44
Other income	10
Operating expenses	(22)
Loss on disposal of non-current assets	**(1)**
Depreciation	**(17)**
Interest expenses	**(2)**
Interest received	**1**
Profit before tax	13
Income tax	(3)
Net profit after tax	10

In the above statement, all the bold lines show non-cash items. Depreciation, for example, is an accounting method for spreading of the cost of a non-current asset over its lifetime. It doesn't actually represent any movement of cash, and so we need to add this amount back on to the profit before tax. This is what is meant by 'adjust for non-cash items'.

Using the indirect method, the purpose is therefore to **adjust for all items in the statement of comprehensive income that do not have any cash effect.**

Note that gains on the disposal of non-current assets will be deducted from profit before tax in the cash flow from operating activities, since they were added in calculating profits in the statement of comprehensive income.

Let's go through these for Success:

- **Depreciation** – this item was deducted from the calculation of profit but no cash transaction was involved, therefore, $17,000 must added back to net profit

- **Loss on disposal of non-current asset** – this item was also deducted from calculating net profit, therefore, $1,000 must be added back

- **Interest received** – we assume that this income may have been generated from an investing activity (which is shown separately), so we remove $1,000 from the net profit before tax, as it was added in the statement of comprehensive income

- **Interest expense** – as with the direct method, this will be deducted in operating cash flow on the bottom lines (after "cash generated from operating activities" - see the final solution for details). This means that we should add $2,000 back to the net profit before tax, at this stage and then take it back off later on.

Here's our cash flow statement so far:

Cash flows from operating activities	31.12.X4
(Indirect method)	**$'000**
Profit before taxation	13
Adjustments for:	
Depreciation	17
Loss on disposal of non-current assets	1
Interest paid	2
Interest received	(1)

So far then, we have $32,000 of cash received from operating activities. We've yet to adjust for the working capital items though, so let's do that next.

3. Calculate the changes in the working capital items of the statement of financial position.

This is calculated by simply comparing the opening and closing balance of each account:

Working Capital Account	Closing Balance	Opening Balance	Difference	Change
Inventory	30	30	-	-
Trade Receivables	60	20	40	Increase
Prepaid operating expenses	3	-	3	Increase
Trade payables	45	25	20	Increase
Accrued operating expenses	3	2	1	Increase

As a general rule, you should remember:

- **When an asset increases that's a cash outflow which is deducted from the cash flow.** For instance, if you buy new inventory for your factory, assets will increase but there will be a cash outflow to pay for them.

- **When as asset decreases it is as cash inflow which is added to the cash flow.** Similarly, if you sell inventory (an asset) then your assets decrease, but cash flows in to the company.

- **When a liability increases it is a cash inflow which is added in the cash flow statement.** Imagine you take out a £1,000 loan. Your liability will increase by the £1,000 debt, but you now have £1,000 in cash available.

- **When a liability decreases it is a cash outflow which is deducted in the cash flow statement.** Conversely, if you pay off your £1,000 debt, your liabilities go down but so does your cash balance in order to pay it off.

Pulling this all together then, we can calculate the cash flow from operating activities using the **indirect** method follows:

Cash flows from operating activities	31.12.X4
(Indirect method)	**$'000**
Profit before taxation	13
Adjustments for:	
Depreciation	17
Loss on disposal of non-current assets	1
Interest paid	2
Interest received	(1)
Working capital changes:	
(Increase)/Decrease in trade receivables	(40)
(Increase)/Decrease in inventories	-
Increase/(Decrease) in prepaid operating expenses	(3)
Increase/(Decrease) in trade payables	20
Increase/(Decrease) in accrued operating expenses	1
Cash generated from operations	**10**
Interest paid	(2)
Income taxes paid	(3)
Net cash from operating activities	**5**

Note that we also added on interest and income taxes paid at the end to get to the final figure. It is worth remembering the following when answering an exam question:

- **Interest paid** is normally **reported within the operating cash flow**, unless otherwise stated in the question

- **Income tax** is normally **classified as operating activity**, unless otherwise stated in the question

Direct vs. Indirect methods

Comparing the direct method with the indirect method, **either method will generate the same results**. The cash flows from operating activities in the above examples generate $5,000 in net operating income using either method.

3.   Cash flow from investing activities

Introduction

Now we move on to the second section of the statement of cash flows: investing activities. **Investing activities generally refer to two main things:**

- **Purchase or disposal of non-current assets** – This is generally a large cash investment in assets that the entity intend to use for several periods in order to make money, such as buildings, machinery, land, etc.

- **Purchase or disposal of shares or bonds** – This is an investment in the sense that the entity will expect to make a financial return in the long-term

Inflows and outflows

Inflows

Examples of cash **inflows** from investing activities are:

- Cash **received** from the **disposal** of property, plant and equipment

- Dividends **received** from a subsidiary entity

- Cash **receipts** from **repayment of loans** made to third parties

Outflows

Examples of cash **outflows** from investing activities are:

- Cash **paid** for the acquisition of property, plant and equipment

- Cash **payments** for the acquisition of other entities

- Cash **payments** for the acquisition interest in joint ventures

Cash flow from investing activities: Example

Success Company serves as a good example to illustrate the calculation of cash flow from investing activities.

Let's take another look at their financial statements:

Success Company	31.12.X4	31.12.X3
Statement of Financial Position	$'000	$'000
Non-current assets		
Tangible assets	85	70
Current assets		
Inventory	30	30
Trade receivables	60	20
Prepaid operating expenses	3	-
Cash in bank and hand	162	135
Total assets	**340**	**255**
Equity & Liabilities		
Issued share capital	70	60
Share premium account	30	20
Revaluation reserve	25	20
Accumulated profits	80	70
	205	170
Non-current liabilities		
Loans	87	58
	87	58
Current liabilities		
Trade payables	45	25
Accrued operating expenses	3	2
	48	27
Total Equity & Liabilities	**340**	**255**

Success Company	31.12.X4
Statement of Comprehensive Income	**$'000**
Sales	140
Cost of goods sold	(96)
Gross profit	44
Other income	10
Operating expenses	(22)
Loss on disposal of non-current assets	(1)
Depreciation	(17)
Interest expenses	(2)
Interest received	1
Profit before tax	13
Income tax	(3)
Net profit after tax	10

Notes:

1. Success disposed of tangible assets in 20X4 with a net book value, $8,000.

Purchase of non-current assets

Let's first start with the cash payments for the purchase of tangible assets.

To calculate the additions we can use the same method that we use when finding incomplete records. This basically involves putting all relevant debits and credits into the accounts and finding the missing figure:

Non-current assets			
Balance b/d	70	Disposals	8
Revaluation	5	Depreciation	17
Cash payments (balance)	**35**	Balance c/d	85
	110		110

So, we know the asset value at the start of the year is $85,000 (a debit) from the SOFP. We also need to include depreciation and disposals on the credit side as these both represent a decrease in value of the asset. On the debit side we also have $5,000 which represents the increase in the revaluation reserve from 20X6 to 20X7. Remember that the revaluation reserve relates to the measurement of non-current assets so as the assets have gone up in value a debit is required.

We therefore conclude that Success has paid $35,000 for purchases of tangible assets. This is a cash outflow and so will appear as a negative figure in the cash flow statement.

Disposal of non-current assets

Success has disposals of assets (see the notes and income statement). We know the net book value was $8,000, but that we made a loss of $1,000 upon sale. That means we must have received $7,000 for it therefore. Here's a proforma you can learn to work this out:

Net book value	$8,000
(Loss)/gain on disposal	($1,000)
Cash received	$7,000

Interest received

Finally, Success has also received interest amounting to $1,000. In the example, it is not mentioned specifically from which activity the interest is received, but we assume that this was generated from an investing activity. In an exam question, you may count interest received as an investing activity, unless otherwise stated in the question.

Cash flows from investing activities

Based on the above, we can now prepare the cash flow from investing activities as follows:

Cash flows from investing activities	31.12.X4
	$'000
Purchase of intangible assets	(35)
Proceeds from disposal of tangible assets	7
Interest received	1
Net cash from investing activities	**(27)**

Success has negative net cash from investing activity, which means an outflow of $27,000 for investing activities. **A decrease in cash from investing activities is fairly usual** since investment is a long-term strategy and often involves a significant cash outflow with no immediate corresponding inflow.

4.   Cash flow from financing activities

Cash flows from financing activities show **how external financing sources have been used by a business** during the reporting period. Cash flows from financing activities are mainly **associated with the long-term liability and equity** items of the balance sheet, such as long term debt and share capital.

Inflows and outflows

Inflows

Examples of **inflows** from financing activities of the entity are:

- Cash **proceeds** from the issuance of new shares

- Cash **receipts** from borrowing from a bank

Outflows

Examples of **outflows** from financing activities of the entity are:

- Cash **payments** to acquire own shares

- Dividends **paid** to shareholders

- Cash **repayments** of amounts borrowed

- Cash **payments** relating to a finance lease (a lease where we have rights over the asset being leased for its whole life)

Cash flow from financing activities: Example

Let's keep going with the Success Company. **We find out the cash movements in relation to financing activities from the equity accounts and long-term borrowings in the statement of comprehensive income.**

Equity cash flows

Under the equity accounts, there is an increase in both the issued share capital and share premium. These changes are straight-forward since we only need to compare the difference between the opening and the closing balance of each account.

Equity Account	Closing Balance	Opening Balance	Difference	Change
Share Capital	70	60	10	Increase
Share Premium	30	20	10	Increase

An increase in the share capital and premium means that shareholders have invested additional funds in the company. Therefore, this is a cash receipt by Success of $20,000 ($10,000 + $10,000).

Liability cash flows

Apart from the changes in the equity accounts, there is also an increase in the loans of Success, by $29,000. Again, **an increase in the loan item means a receipt of money from the bank**, from a cash point of view.

On the basis of the above, we may prepare the cash flow from financing activities as follows:

Cash flows from financing activities	31.12.X4
	$'000
Proceeds of share issue	20
Proceeds from long-term borrowings	29
Net cash from financing activities	**49**

5. The Statement of Cash Flows: Full Statement

Having prepared the cash flow from all three activities of Success, we may now put them altogether to prepare the entire cash flow statement of the company. The cash flow statement of Success is presented below using indirect method.

Success Company		31.12.X4
Statement of Cash Flows for the year ended 31 Dec 2014	$'000	$'000
Cash flows from operating activities		
Profit before taxation	13	
Adjustments for:		
Depreciation	17	
Loss on disposal of non-current assets	1	
Interest paid	2	
Interest received	(1)	
Working capital changes:		
(Increase)/Decrease in trade receivables	(40)	
(Increase)/Decrease in inventories	-	
Increase/(Decrease) in prepaid operating expenses	(3)	
Increase/(Decrease) in trade payables	20	
Increase/(Decrease) in accrued operating expenses	1	
Cash generated from operations	**10**	
Interest paid	(2)	
Income taxes paid	(3)	
Net cash from operating activities		**5**
Cash flows from investing activities		
Purchase of intangible assets	(35)	
Proceeds from disposal of tangible assets	7	
Interest received	1	
Net cash from investing activities		**(27)**
Cash flows from financing activities		
Proceeds of share issue	20	
Proceeds from long-term borrowings	29	
Net cash from financing activities		**49**
Net increase in cash and cash equivalents		**27**
Cash and cash equivalents at 1ˢᵗ Jan 20X4		**135**
Cash and cash equivalents at 31ˢᵗ Dec 20X4		**162**

astranti
financial training

The bottom line

The bottom of the cash flow operates as **a reconciliation of bank balances**, including the balances at the beginning and end of the year as well as the net movement in cash during the year. Therefore, by adding the cash flow result of each activity, we calculate the net cash movement during the year, in this case, $27,000. Adding this amount to the opening bank balance of Success, $135,000, we end at $162,000 which reconciles with the closing balance of the bank of Success, as per the statement of financial position.

6.   Importance of the statement of cash flows

You may be wondering what exactly is the point of a statement of cash flows. The income statement seems like an obvious statement, and the SoFP is pretty useful. Those are all good, but why do we need this other statement that seems to be neither here nor there? Well, **here are a few reason why the Statement of Cash Flows is an important financial statement.**

Liquidity and solvency

The cash flow statement **helps users to assess liquidity and solvency**. A good cash position is very important to a company in the short term in order to ensure the survival of the business, and to enable debts and dividends to be paid. Good cash flow means that a company can pay for things without having funds tied up in capital and investments.

Adaptability

The cash flow statement can enable users to **assess financial adaptability**. It helps the user answer questions regarding their **ability to move with the times**. Will the entity be able to take effective action to alter its cash flows in response to any unexpected events? Let's say a recession hits. If the company is short of cash, or has even been losing cash in previous years then it would seem unlikely to be able to see through the recession unless it obtains new funding. The question then is: **if an unexpected cost comes in, does the company have the ability to deal with it?**

Future cash flow

It can help the users assess future cash flows. **An adequate cash position in the longer term is vital to allow asset replacement, repayment of debt and to fund further expansion.** Users will use recent cash flow information to help them assess future cash flows.

Cash generation

The cash flow helps to **highlight where cash is being generated**. The cash flow statement will examine cash that is being generated from the core activities of the business and other non-operating activities. Therefore, a company knows where to focus their attention if they need a cash boost.

CIMA BA3 Study Text

Chapter 15

Interpreting Financial Statements

1. Introduction

In this final chapter, we will go back to where we started and **look at what exactly makes a financial statement a useful piece of information**. In the preceding chapters we have looked at all sorts of ways to produce and edit financial statements, and now we look at what they are used to show.

Interpreting financial statements

Financial statements are all well and good, but they only really show final figures for profits, capital, assets and things like that. With these final figures, do we really get any sense of how well the business is performing? Is it doing better or worse than the competition? Is it better or worse than it was one year ago? How much profit can I expect to make from investment?

These are all questions that shareholders, owners and directors want to know, but before we can answer them, we need to make the information provided in the financial statement relevant to the people who have access to it.

Calculating ratios

A ratio is simply a comparison of two figures. So, for example, the ratio of apples to oranges in my fruit bowl is 2:1, because I have 4 apples and two oranges. So, for every orange, I have two apples.

So, with regards to the world of business, we can use ratios to compare figures, which ultimately gives us an idea of the internal workings of the business. However, the ratios alone are rarely very informative. **The real function of calculating ratios is to use them for comparison with other periods, other businesses, budgets or official statistics.** These comparisons give us context for the relative success of the business. In this section, we will consider **4 main types of ratios**:

- **Profitability (performance)**

- **Liquidity (solvency)**

- **Efficiency (use of assets)**

- **Capital structure (gearing)**

2. Example financial statements

We'll use the following example financial statements to work out a range of ratios. For the moment you can skip over this, but do refer back to them for each ratio so you understand where the numbers come from.

Income statement for 31st December 20X6

	£	£
Sales		42,930
Opening inventories	7,500	
Purchases	12,340	
	19,840	
Closing inventories	(1,840)	
Cost of sales		(18,000
Gross profit		24,930
Expenses		(6,810)
Operating profit		18,120
Interest payable on loan		(720)
Profit before tax		17,400
Income tax		(1,750)
Profit for period		15,650

Statement of financial position for 31st December 20X6

Assets	£	£
Non-current assets		21,536
Current assets		
Inventories	1,840	
Receivables	4,220	
Bank	10,720	
Cash	5,014	
		21,794
		43,330
Equity and liabilities		
Equity		34,280
Non-current liabilities		
Bank loan		7,200
Current liabilities		
Payables		1,850
		43,330

astranti
financial training

3. Profitability ratios

Gross profit margin

$$\frac{\text{Gross profit}}{\text{Sales}} \times 100 \quad = \text{Gross profit margin}$$

So, using the our figures we get:

$$\frac{24{,}930}{42{,}930} \times 100 \quad = 58.1\%$$

So, we have a gross profit margin of **58.1%**, which means that **for every £1 of sales, approximately 58p of that pound remained in the business** for expenses, possible dividends, retention of profit, etc.

This ratio is usually used for self-comparison over time. So, if the gross profit margin for the previous year had been **62%**, contrasting that with the current figure shows a decrease. This could be cause my any number of reasons:

- Sales revenue decreased.

- Sales revenue stayed constant but costs increased.

- Prices were kept steady to keep market share, despite rising costs.

- Suppliers increased price/stopped discounts.

All of these changes are measurable either in price change or volume change. The gross profit margin, then, measures the effectiveness of the sales team, pricing and purchasing or a business.

Gross profit mark-up

$$\frac{\text{Gross profit}}{\text{Cost of sales}} \times 100 \quad = \text{Gross profit mark-up}$$

Using our figures, we get:

$$\frac{24{,}930}{18{,}000} \times 100 \quad = 139\%$$

So, that means for every £1 spend on purchasing goods, we added value of approximately **£1.39** to make **£2.39**.

Operating profit margin

$$\frac{\text{Operating profit}}{\text{Sales}} \times 100 \quad = \text{Operating profit margin}$$

So, for us, that will be:

$$\frac{18,120}{42,930} \times 100 \quad = 42.2\%$$

The percentage **42.2%** doesn't really mean much on its own. But this ratio is useful for comparison with other organisations and the industry average to get an idea of performance.

Return on capital ratios

This ratio measures the earnings generated per £1 of capital, and so it is generally of interest to investors of a company.

There are several ways to calculate this ratio, but we will look at two:

- **Return on capital employed (ROCE)**

- **Return on equity (ROE)**

Return on equity obviously just uses a figure for equity, but capital employed is the sum of equity and non-current liabilities, such as long term loans.

Sometimes, the equity figure is taken as an average throughout the year, since yearly activity in equity will alter calculations. Return in this context essentially means profit, and so this figure will depend on whether we use **ROCE** or **ROE**.

ROCE

$$\frac{\text{Operating profit}}{\text{Average capital employed by shareholders and lenders}} \times 100 \quad = \text{ROCE}$$

This ratio tells us the profit available as a percentage of the capital.

The 'average capital employed' figure is calculated in the following way:

astranti
financial training

Closing capital employed	(34,280 + 7,200)	= 41,480
Opening capital employed	(41,480 – 15,650)	= 25,830
		67,310

67,310 divided by 2 = **33,655**, which is the average capital employed.

So, putting in these figures we get:

$$\frac{18,120}{33,655} \times 100 = 53.8\%$$

Which gives us a return of **53.8%**, which tells us how much of the capital is available as profit.

ROE

$$\frac{\text{Profit for the period}}{\text{Average equity}} \times 100 = \text{ROE}$$

This ratio tells us the profit available only to shareholders as a percentage of their funds. It is sometimes known as return on net assets. The average equity figure is calculated in the following way:

Closing equity		= 34,280
Opening equity	(34,280 – 15,650)	= 18,630
		52,910

52,910 divided by 2 = **26,455**, which is the average equity.

Putting in our figures we get:

$$\frac{15,650}{26,455} \times 100 = 59.2\%$$

Which gives us a return on net assets of **59.2%**.

4. Liquidity ratios

Liquidity ratios, also known as solvency ratios, measure the ability of a company to pay their payables.

The current ratio (working capital ratio)

This ratio simply compares current assets with current liabilities:

$$\frac{\text{Current assets}}{\text{Current liabilities}} = \text{Current ratio}$$

Let's plug in our numbers:

$$\frac{21{,}794}{1{,}850} = 11.8$$

The result is a ratio that tells us for every £1 of debt, we have £11.80 in assets available to pay it off.

We have quite a high current ratio, which might mean that we are holding too much in assets (like inventories or cash), which is money that could be used more efficiently elsewhere.

Quick ratio (acid test ratio)

$$\frac{\text{Current assets - inventories}}{\text{Current liabilities}} = \text{Quick ratio}$$

This is an alternative to the current ratio, and is used when inventories take a long time to become cash (low liquidity). Using our figures we get:

$$\frac{19{,}954}{1{,}850} = 10.8$$

5. Efficiency ratios

Efficiency ratios measure the use of assets.

Asset turnover ratios

This ratio simply compares the sales revenue to the value of assets. So, it can tell us how much profit is made from certain assets.

$$\frac{\text{Sales revenue}}{\text{Assets}} = £\text{...}$$

We can use any combination of assets as the denominator. Let's take non-current assets as our example:

$$\frac{42,930}{21,536} = £1.99$$

So, for every **£1** invested in non-current assets, the business made **£1.99**.

Inventories days

$$\frac{\text{Inventories}}{\text{Cost of sales}} \times 365 = \text{Inventories days}$$

This ratio tells us the average number of days that an item spends in inventories. Using our figures we get:

$$\frac{1,840}{18,000} \times 365 = 37 \text{ days}$$

We round the number of days to the nearest whole number, and find that an item spends an average of **37 days** in the inventories.

Obviously, we just used the closing inventories figure. It might be necessary to calculate an average inventories figure (opening + closing, divided by 2).

For a manufacturing company, this figure should match the average production cycle for a product.

If this number is high, then the business probably have too much in the way of inventories, and could be spending the money elsewhere. Equally, if the number is low, it is likely that the business are stocking insufficient amounts of inventory.

Again, this is a number more useful for comparison with other companies.

Inventories turnover

We can calculate the inventories turnover as the amount of times an item is bought and sold. Obviously, this does not mean that an item does go back and forth, but **it shows how many times an item could be sold in a period.**

$$\frac{\text{Cost of sales}}{\text{Average inventories}} = \frac{18,000}{4,670} = 3.9$$

Receivables days

This ratio gives us the average amount of time it takes customers to settle debts.

$$\frac{\text{Receivables}}{\text{Sales}} \times 365 = \text{Receivables days}$$

For our figures, we find:

$$\frac{4,220}{42,930} \times 365 = 36 \text{ days}$$

Payables days

Similarly to receivables days, **this ratio tells us how long it takes the business to pay back debts on average.**

$$\frac{\text{Payables}}{\text{Purchases}} \times 365 = \text{Payables days}$$

$$\frac{1,850}{12,340} \times 365 = 55 \text{ days}$$

This ratio, as with receivables days, are best compared with previous figures to show trends.

Total working capital ratio

This ratio tells us the length of time that capital is tied up in inventories, receivables, and payables, before being available as profit. Therefore, it just the total of the previous 3 ratios:

(Inventories + Receivables) – Payables = Total working capital days

= (37 + 36) – 55 = **18 days.**

6.   Capital structure ratios

Gearing ratio (leverage ratio)

This ratio gives us the relationship between externally provided finance (from loans, etc.) and the total capital employed. It informs us about the amount of risk involved in adopted financing strategies.

$$\frac{\text{Debt}}{\text{Total capital employed}} \times 100 \quad = \text{Gearing ratio}$$

A higher percentage here means that more profits have to be earned in order to pay interest costs on borrowing, and thus it is a more risky investment. Our figures give us:

$$\frac{7,200}{41,480} \times 100 \quad = 17.4$$

We can use the same method with equity to find the debt: equity **ratio:**

$$\frac{\text{Debt}}{\text{Equity}} \times 100 \quad = \text{Debt: Equity ratio}$$

$$\frac{7,200}{34,280} \times 100 \quad = 21$$

This shows how much debt an organisation is using to fund their operations relative to how much equity they are using. The higher debt : equity ratio the more debt is being used and, therefore, the greater the risk. This is because they have used an aggressive financing strategy utilising debt.

astranti
financial training

Interest cover

The interest cover measures the number of times that profit can cover fixed-interest on long term loans. It is a measure of the security of a payment, since a high number will show that a loan is payable.

$$\frac{\text{Operating profit}}{\text{Interest payable}} = \text{Interest cover}$$

$$\frac{18,120}{720} = 25$$

So our operating profit could pay back loan interest **25 times**.

7. Ratio comparison

Without some fair comparison the figures are themselves largely meaningless. There is no one right figure for either working capital or liquidity ratios and what is acceptable can vary significantly between industries.

As an example, the supermarket industry typically operates with a current ratio of less than one and a negative cash operating cycle.

The reason is that with long payables days (due to their supplier power) and the need to sell products quickly to avoid wastage, they typically receive money from customers before they need to pay their creditors for the purchase of those goods. Supermarkets are typically cash rich therefore.

Conversely a manufacturing company will often have high levels of raw materials, work in progress and finished goods, and give good payment terms to their customers, resulting in a long cash operating cycle. If they had a current ratio less than one it would probably indicate that they were in serious difficulty.

It is typical therefore to compare the results with some other standard:

- Past Performance - Across historical time periods for the same firm (the last 5 years for example)

- Against budgets (were results as predicted?)

- Between similar firms in the same industry

- Between other similar divisions of the business

astranti
financial training

Having made a comparison, it is crucial that possible meanings of those comparisons are evaluated. In the examples above we have speculated about the possible reasons for the changes in ratios – the real reasons must be ascertained and conclusions drawn to help ensure a good liquidity position in the future.

8.   Integrated reporting

Introduction

American social philosopher Eric Hoffer once said 'the only way to predict the future is to have the power to shape the future'. Well, as far as investors are concerned, the best way to predict the future of a business is to check out its integrated report.

Integrated reports help investors, people who buy shares in a business, to predict **how companies will perform in the future**. The report does this by using data from the financial statements - which show their past and present performance – as well as information on their key performance indicators (more on these later). This prediction allows investors to decide whether or not to buy shares in a company.

The Integrated Report

So far we have mainly looked at the historical position of the business, as part of our financial reporting which gives investors an accurate picture of how the business has performed up until the present day.

However, **investors and other users of the financial statements are likely to be interested in how a company will perform in the future.**

In 2013, **the International Integrated Reporting Council** – which arose from the need for a **clear and comparable framework for integrated reports** – provided an official definition of what an integrated report is.

This definition basically explains that integrated reports should combine information about a company and its performance with **forward-looking information** (information about and plans for the company's future), in order to understand **how the company currently creates value**, and how they will **create value in the future**.

Value Creation

Now, in that previous explanation, we mentioned the concept of value creation. Let's just look at what value creation actually means, in order to help you better understand what investors want to see in integrated reports.

If a product has **value**, it means that the product **meets not only the needs, but also the desires of the customer**. It gives them something that is **worth more than the sum of all the processes involved in its construction**.

In other words, when a retail business sells a t-shirt, it provides the customer with an object which is worth more to them than the total cost associated with making the t-shirt, such as the materials, the wages for staff, the electricity to power the t-shirt pressing machines, etc.

Because of this, businesses can justify selling products for a **profit** - that is, more money than they cost to make.

A common example of **good value creation is the construction of a successful brand name.** As I'm sure you know, a product from a well-known brand (Gucci for example) holds more value to a customer than a product which is essentially the same from a lesser-known or lesser-respected brand. This is why customers are willing to pay more money for the same products from these brands.

When looking at an **integrated report**, investors want to see that **a company has the means, the experience and the audience to continue creating value, that customers are willing to pay for.**

If there is an increase in the value of the products or services offered by the company, the price that an investor will be willing to pay for shares is also likely to increase. This means the shares held by investors will become more valuable in themselves as the investor will now gain a bigger profit when he eventually sells these shares.

Therefore, if an investor looks at an integrated report and finds that a company is likely to continue and increase their value creation, this will encourage the investor to invest.

Principles of an Integrated Report

The framework that is provided by the IIRC sets out:

- **guiding principles** – the way the report should be produced

- **content elements** – what it should contain

Because there are these international standards, integrated reports should be easy for users to understand and compare.

Who uses integrated reports?

The IR Framework is **primarily aimed at companies listed on stock markets,** however that doesn't mean that other kinds of entities cannot utilise it where it is appropriate – integrated reports can be helpful for all kinds of businesses!

The main individuals who use the information provided in integrated reports are the **providers of financial capital** – in other words, investors. But, just as the financial reports can be useful for several different interest groups (employees, suppliers, customers etc), so can integrated reports!

Key performance indicators (KPIs)

Key Performance Indicators are an important part of integrated reports, as they help investors to see how well a business has been achieving its goals.

They are basically **metrics (standardised measurements) that are decided upon by companies, which help them to measure their overall performance.**

Key Performance Indicators are subjective, and are decided on based upon specific the goals of the particular business.

For example, a company operating a call centre might have a plan which involves expanding by growing its client base. So here, the KPIs might be something like this:

- Average number of calls handled per operator per day

- Average call-waiting time

- Customer satisfaction with call outcomes

- Client satisfaction with services offered

These might be **compared with targets**. For example, with the average call-waiting time, a business might decide that in order to achieve their goal of client-base growth, over 2 minute waiting time per call is bad, under 2 minutes is good and under 1 minute is ideal. All of these measurements can help the company figure out how well they are achieving the goal of growing their client base.

Principles-based

The IR Framework is **principles-based** and therefore **it does not dictate specific KPIs to be disclosed in the reports.** As we have just seen, it would be inappropriate for the framework to stipulate specific KPIs, since these are always specific to individual companies and their goals.

Which KPIs to include in the report must instead be **decided on by senior management**. It is up to the senior management to ensure they report issues which are relevant to the business's performance and important for an investor to see. A range of **financial AND non-financial** KPIs should be reported.

We know that it is important for the Integrated Report to be strategically-focused and concerned with future performance, rather than focusing solely on past financial information. It is with this aim in mind that management should decide on KPIs. Our call centre's strategy is based around increasing customer numbers and so the KPIs should be focused on metrics which measure that key goal.

Capitals

The Integrated Reporting framework needs to be reported in relation to different **'capitals'**.

These are different **categories of resources that are used by a business to help it achieve its goals**. The capitals that are mentioned in the integrated reporting framework are as follows:

Financial

Money that is available within a company or from external sources.

Human

Management and staff.

Natural

Natural resources that a company may use in its activities. These are often decreased in a way that leads to an increase in financial capital (profit). e.g. materials used to produce products which are then sold.

Natural capital comes in two forms:

- Renewable – Such as vegetables and other crops

- Non-renewable – Such as land and minerals

Intellectual

Intangible assets such as patents and copyrights.

Manufactured

Assets manufactured by an entity, either for sale or for retention

Social and Relationship

Stakeholder relationships and the development of shared values within a firm that help it to succeed e.g. a competitive culture in an investment bank.

The integrated report **needs to report on** the value creation process, and therefore **increase or decrease in the different kinds of capital.** For example when a business buys the materials to make a product, its financial capital decreases. However, it has gained manufactured intellectual capital, in the form of a product held for sale.

Content of an Integrated Report

As we have mentioned, a company should be using their integrated reports to consider long-term value creation, rather than just reporting on how they have performed in the past!

Below is a summarised list of all the elements that an Integrated Report should contain, according to the International Integrated Reporting Framework:

- A review of the **outside factors** which have an impact on the workings of the business and value creation, e.g. legal, commercial and political factors

- The way the business is **managed and run** (governance) and how this impacts on **value creation**

- The company's **plan for success** (business model)

- **Uncertainties** that the business faces (**risks**), and plans it has to respond to these (**opportunities**)

- Information on how a company **uses its resources or capitals to achieve its goals**

- To what extent the company has **achieved** its goals so far

- What **challenges** the business is likely to encounter and how these could change the business's plans

- **How a company decides on which information to include** in the report and how this shows it has taken account of the integrated reporting guidance

CIMA BA3 Study Text

Chapter 16

Capital Structure

1. Capital markets

A capital market (also known as a **stock market**, or **stock exchange**) is a way of looking at the capital of an entity as a purchasable commodity. Think of it as a giant supermarket, and on the shelves of each aisle are small portions of the capital of any business. **Each small portion of capital is a share,** and when you purchase it from the supermarket, you then own a small portion of that business.

Companies can raise money by selling these small parts of their company to investors. You could sell 1 share for £10, where 1 share equates to 0.01% of the business. This would mean that 100% of the business would be worth £100,000.

But, if you sell 100% of the business, then you are no longer an owner, and so it wouldn't be your business any more! So, if you take your business to a capital market, then **in order retain control and ownership, you will need to maintain at least 51% of the company** as that gives you voting rights to make key decisions in shareholder meetings.

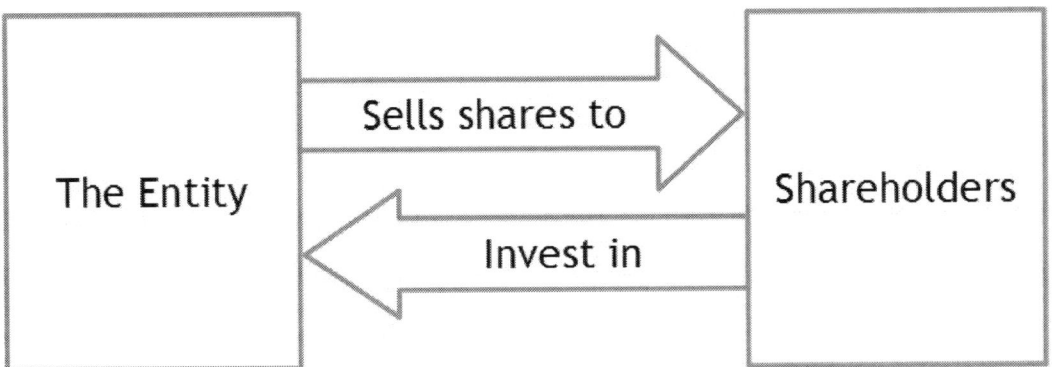

On 18th September 2014, Chinese e-commerce company Alibaba listed on the New York Stock Exchange for the first time, raising close to $22bn of funds, the largest initial public offering of shares in the world at that time. After the launch, as share prices soared, Alibaba's founder became China's richest man worth an estimated $16bn.

On the downside, at that point Ma owned just 6% of the company he had founded. Yes, he was wealthy, but now he had shareholders to answer to. That's something that doesn't suit every business owner. Some years after Richard Branson floated his company Virgin on the stock market he bought the company back because he wanted to regain control.

2.   Equity finance

An equity investment refers to the buying and holding of shares on a stock market by individuals or firms.

So, what's in it for an investor? They'll need to make a return from their investment to make it worthwhile. Well, there are two main ways in which an equity investment will do this:

Dividends – this is an amount of the profits made by the company, which is paid to shareholders, and;

Capital gains – this is the increase in value of the share over time.

Ordinary shares (or 'common stock')

Ordinary shares are the most common type of share. This is the kind of share most people think of when they talk about owning stock in a company, and is essentially your basic, lowest-level share.

Dividends

Dividends are only payable at the discretion of the directors and are not compulsory. This means that the share could only make money for the investor by increasing in value, and that depends on many other factors. Thus, there is no guarantee that a share will make the investor any money, and it may in fact cost them money instead!

Winding up

Ordinary shares generally have the lowest priority in recovering their investment in the event of 'winding up' (this essentially means dissolving the company by selling assets and paying off debts, or 'going into liquidation'). This means the ordinary shareholders will be re-compensated last, and potentially face losing their investment if the business has insufficient funds.

Voting rights

Ordinary shareholders are the owners of the company and receive voting rights, meaning that they can vote on issues raised at shareholder meetings. This can include electing directors and members of the board.

Risk

All of this means that ordinary shares are the most risky of all types of investment in a company. For this reason, investors require a high return on their investment in the company to cover the risks involved. If there are no dividends or the share price doesn't increase, then the investor will look elsewhere.

Preference shares (or preferred stock)

A preference share (or preferred stock), is a share that gives the holder a number of beneficial rights over holders of common shares.

Dividends

When a company declares a dividend, they are obliged to pay preference shareholders before they pay those who own ordinary shares. So, in this instance, preference shares are preferable to ordinary shares.

In addition to this, preference shares usually carry a fixed dividend. This means that if a company sells preference shares, then they will be obliged to declare and pay dividends to these shareholders at regular intervals (usually annually). It also means that if the company starts doing really well, the preference shareholders won't benefit because they continue getting the same payment year in, year out.

Winding up

In the event of a winding up or liquidation of the company, preference shares have a higher priority than ordinary shares, so an investor is more likely to recover their investment in this case. However, preference shares are subordinate to debt or bonds (we will take a look at these in a later section) so they'll only get paid once after other debt is paid off.

Voting rights

A preference share usually carries no voting rights, so preference shareholders are unable to vote in shareholder meetings on important issues regarding the company (such as electing directors).

Risk

This means that preference shares are generally a lower risk than ordinary shares, but will also be at a higher cost than ordinary shares. This means returns are more likely, but that they will probably be smaller.

Status

Preference shares function in a specific way that make them more like a bond (which is a kind of debt finance). Therefore, **preference shares are considered to be a hybrid instrument, because they have elements of both equity and debt** (e.g. preference shares can be 'converted' into debt – more in this soon!).

	Ordinary shares	Preference shares
Dividends	Not compulsory	Usually carry fixed dividend
Priority (winding-up)	Lowest priority	Higher priority (subordinate to debt)
Voting rights	Yes	No
Risk	Higher	Lower than ordinary shares (but higher than debt)
Other	Basic/common stock	Convertible, hybrid instrument

Types of preference share

There are four kinds of preference share, and they all work in slightly different ways.

Cumulative preference shares

The name 'cumulative' comes from the fact that **these shares receive a regular dividend from the issuing company, and these payments must be paid no matter what.**

So, imagine you have cumulative preference shares in Lemon Plc, and they pay a fixed dividend every year on their preference shares. In year 1, year 2 and year 3, you receive your dividend as usual. But, in year 4, Lemon Plc declare a dividend, but it isn't paid (sometimes this does happen). And then, the same thing happens in year 5.

Now in year 6, things are back to normal and you receive the fixed dividend for that year. But, because you have cumulative preference shares, the company must pay you for year 4 and year 5, too, and so in year 6 you receive dividends for years 4, 5 and 6.

Thus, the name comes from the fact that your dividend payment accumulates each year, even if it isn't paid.

Non-cumulative preference shares

These shares are just like cumulative preference shares, except **the company doesn't have to pay you for previous periods where you didn't receive a dividend.**

So, using the example with Lemon Plc, you would only receive a dividend in years 1, 2, 3 and 6, and nothing for years 4 and 5.

Participating preference shares

This type of preference share gives the holder the opportunity to earn extra dividend income based on the company hitting certain targets. So if you had participating preference shares in Lemon Plc, and they declare that a proportion of the profits of the new subsidiary Orange Plc will be paid to participating shareholders in the form of a dividend, then you will receive your usual fixed dividend AND the extra 'preferred' dividend from Orange Plc, whereas other preference share would only receive the fixed dividend.

Convertible preference shares

Convertible preference shares are shares that give the holder the right to convert the preference share to an ordinary share at a later date. So, if you have convertible preference shares in Lemon Plc, and you decide that you'd like to have a vote in the company shareholder meetings, then you may want to exercise your right to convert your share to common stock.

3. Debt finance

A debt investment is a way for a company to raise finance without losing any ownership. Rather than selling portions of the capital, the company are essentially selling a promise to repay a fixed amount (with interest) at a future date.

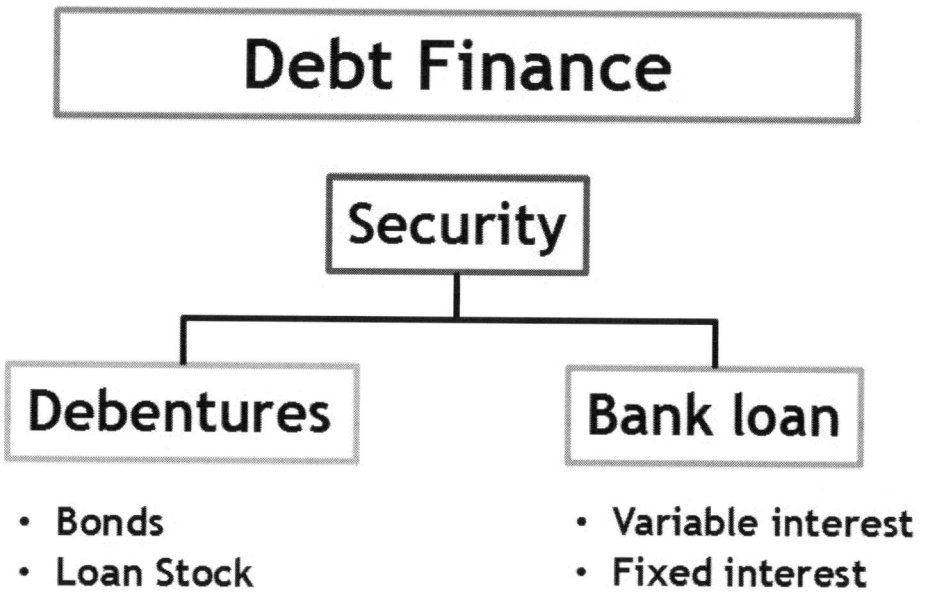

Security

A security is a way for a lender to protect themselves from losing the money they have loaned in the event that the person to whom they lent money cannot repay their debts.

It's like leaving your credit card with the waiting staff at a bar. Rather than paying for all of your drinks each time you order, you can start a 'tab' and add the cost of the drinks to that, paying the cumulative total at the end of the night.

But, from the bar's perspective, they want to make sure you stick around and pay the tab at the end of the night, rather than just running off without paying! And, they want to make sure you actually do have the money to pay, so they will take a credit card – which will guarantee payment – as a **security to ensure that the debt is paid for** at the end of the night.

Most commonly the security used to support a loan is in the form of **property or other valuable assets which can be sold should the loan not be paid off.**

Fixed and floating charge

When it comes to securing debt finance, **there are two main kinds of security (or 'charge') that can be used.**

A fixed charge secures a debt against a specific asset, such as land or buildings. This would mean that, in the event that the company defaults on the loan, the debtor would gain ownership of the specific assets (land or a building).

This is the **less risky option**, since a fixed asset is clearly redeemable by the debtor, regardless of the financial position of the company after defaulting on debts.

A floating charge secures a debt against 'general' assets, so there is no specific asset. This would mean that the debtor would gain ownership of the company's general assets until the debt is repaid. This is a riskier option, since it is uncertain what assets will be in the company should it not pay its debt.

Debentures, bonds, or loan stock

A debenture is a **medium to long-term debt instrument used by large companies to borrow money.** The term is used interchangeably with **bond, loan stock** or **note.** A debenture is thus like a loan evidencing the fact that **the company is liable to pay a specified amount with interest.**

Debentures are generally **freely transferable** by the debenture holder and **may be traded on an exchange.** Debenture holders have **no rights to vote** in the company's general meetings of shareholders, but they may have separate meetings or votes e.g. on changes to the rights attached to the debentures.

The interest paid by the company on a debenture is called a **coupon.**

Convertible debentures

Convertible debentures are debentures which can be converted into equity shares of the issuing company after a pre-determined period of time. In this regard, they are similar to convertible preference shares.

"Convertibility" is a feature that companies may add to the bonds they issue to make them more attractive to buyers. For example, if you own a convertible bond, and you see that the company's share price is growing, you can convert your bond to a share, and make a profit on the increasing share price.

As a result of the benefit of being able to convert, convertible bonds typically have **lower interest rates** than non-convertible corporate bonds. This means that the investor will receive less from the company in interest, which is better for the company, and worse for the investor.

4. Rights and bonus issues

Rights issue

A rights issue is **an issue of additional new shares by a company to raise funds where existing shareholders have the privilege to buy a specified number of new shares from the firm at a specified price within a specified time.**

By first offering shares to existing shareholders, a company can raise finance (receive money from shareholders) from their current shareholders without those shareholders diluting their stake in the company (i.e. they keep the same percentage of ownership of the company). A rights issue is thus **in contrast to an initial public offering, where shares are issued to the general public through market exchanges.**

For example, say a company offers a 5:1 rights issue, which gives all shareholders the right (but not the obligation) to buy one share for every five shares they already own. The new share can be bought for 50p, whereas existing shares are £1.

If there are 100,000 shareholders with 5 shares each and each of them exercises their rights, then the company will receive 50p x 100,000 = £50,000 in new funds.

The **shareholders also retain their percentage stake in the company**. Previously, there were 100,000 shareholders with 5 shares each, which makes 500,000 shares in issue. Each shareholder owned 5 out of 500,000 shares, which is 0.00001% of the company. After the rights issue there are 600,000 shares in issue, which each shareholder have 6 shares, which is again 0.00001%.

Bonus issue

A bonus issue (also known as capitalisation issue or scrip issue) is a 'free' issue of shares to existing shareholders. As such, no fresh capital enters the business from investment, and no further earnings are generated.

The issue would be calculated relative to existing holdings. This means that, for example, one new 'scrip' share may be issued for every ten shares currently owned.

The company issuing the scrip shares has now expanded the number of shares in existence but not increased the value of the company. This means that the relative value of each pre-existing share has been reduced slightly.

There are few real benefits of a bonus issue either to the company or shareholders. The problem is that although more shares are in issue the intrinsic value of the company stays the same meaning that each share is simply worth a little less. Companies may sometimes do this if they don't have many shares in issue and the price is high making them hard to buy or sell. e.g. Company X is worth £1m and has 100 shares in issue worth $10,000 each so people are be put off buying just 1 share due to the cost.

By having a bonus issue so that there are 10,000 shares, each share is now worth just $100 meaning people can invest in Company X with lower amounts making them more marketable.

Considerations

Deciding whether or not to offer a rights or bonus issue is a serious decision for the management of a company. **Below are a list of the key considerations involved:**

Engaging a broker to manage the offering processes

One negative of an issue is the added bureaucracy and cost of working with brokers to arrange and manage the process. Unlike other methods of finance, such as bank loans or private equity, an issue will depend on co-operation with stock market exchanges, and this can be costly and time-consuming.

However, given that an issue requires that a company already has shareholders, then dealing with brokers and exchanges may not be a significant problem for a company that has been listed for a number of years already.

Subscription price per new share

For a rights issue, the price of additional shares is often at a discount to current prices to encourage shareholders to take up their rights. **If the discount is too low, then the rights issue will raise less finance** for the company, which is one of the main reasons a company would seek to offer a rights issue in the first place.

A low discount price may also be seen to **undervalue the company**, since they are selling their stock at a much lower price than the listed market value. This can have a negative impact on market perceptions, which may actually cause the value of the stock to decrease.

Number of new shares to be sold

Financial managers will need to consider how many new shares are to be offered to existing shareholders. **The key here is getting the right balance between raising enough finance for the company, without giving up a significant percentage of ownership, and also without diluting the shares of existing shareholders.**

The effect of an issue on the value of the current shares

Rights and bonus issues almost always have a measurable impact on the market price of shares in issue.

This is because shares offered at a discount or for free added to the existing shares at market value will average out to a lower figure. Thus, the bigger the discount the greater the dilution in price of all shares after issue.

On the other hand, the **market value of shares can increase if the finance raised is used effectively by the company**. If the new funds are well-invested, then this will increase the value of the company. This will have the positive effect of increasing the share price.

The impact on existing shareholders

A rights issue can have a negative impact on existing shareholders if they do not exercise their rights.

Lemon Plc has 100 shareholders, who collectively own 25% of the company. Each shareholder has 10 shares at a market value of £1 per share, and so there are 1,000 shares in issue. This means that any given shareholder individually owns 1% of the shares in issue.

Now, Lemon Plc offer a rights issue of 2:1, effectively giving all shareholders the option to purchase 2 new shares for every existing share. This would then mean that there would be 3,000 shares in issue if everyone exercised their rights.

If only 99 shareholders exercise their right, then they would own 2,970 of the shares between them (30 each). However, the 1 shareholder who didn't exercise their right still only has 10 shares out of 2,980. This individual would now only have around 0.3% of the shares in issue, thus their stake has been reduced.

5. Dividends

Accounting for dividends

As mentioned, **dividends are the amounts paid to shareholders from an entity's profit**. In other words, they are **not an expense**, but a distribution of profits among the owners. Different types of share will come with different rights and so the amount received by the shareholder will depend on what type and how many shares are held.

Dividends are usually split into two payments:

- **Interim dividend** – this is an amount paid during the year

- **Final dividend** - this is the amount paid after the end of the year

In the financial statements **dividends are only accounted for in the year they are paid**. This is because the final dividend is often not known until after the current period year end as directors can only calculate it once the final profit for the year is calculated.

As a result, it is most common that **a company will show dividends paid in the financial statements as the final dividend from the previous period and the interim dividend from the current period.**

For example, if we have the following dividends for the years X1 and X2:

	20X1	20X2
Interim dividend	£100	£150
Final dividend	£200	£250
Total	£300	£400

In the 20X2 financial statements the following are disclosed:

Final dividend 20X1 (paid in 20X2)	£200
Interim dividend 20X2	£150
Total dividends paid in 20X2	£350

The £350 is the dividends actually paid during the year. This will be **shown in the statement of changes in equity** in the financial statements.

CIMA BA3 Study Text

Chapter 17

Tables and Formulae

Present Value Tables

Present value of £1 i.e. $(1 + r)^{-1}n$ where r = interest rate, n = number of periods until payment or receipt.

Periods (n)	Interest rates (r)									
	1%	2%	3%	4%	5%	6%	7%	8%	9%	10%
1	.990	.980	.971	.962	.962	.943	.935	.926	.917	.909
2	.980	.961	.943	.925	.907	.890	.873	.857	.842	.826
3	.971	.942	.915	.889	.864	.840	.816	.794	.772	.751
4	.961	.924	.888	.855	.823	.792	.763	.735	.708	.683
5	.951	.906	.863	.822	.784	.747	.713	.681	.650	.621
6	.942	.888	.837	.790	.746	.705	.666	.630	.596	.564
7	.933	.871	.813	.760	.711	.665	.623	.583	.547	.513
8	.923	.853	.789	.731	.677	.627	.582	.540	.502	.467
9	.914	.837	.766	.703	.645	.592	.544	.500	.460	.424
10	.905	.820	.744	.676	.614	.558	.508	.463	.422	.386
11	.896	.804	.722	.650	.585	.527	.475	.429	.388	.350
12	.887	.788	.701	.625	.557	.497	.444	.397	.356	.319
13	.879	.773	.681	.601	.530	.469	.415	.368	.326	.290
14	.870	.758	.661	.577	.505	.442	.388	.340	.299	.263
15	.861	.743	.642	.555	.481	.417	.362	.315	.275	.239
16	.853	.728	.623	.534	.458	.394	.339	.292	.252	.218
17	.844	.714	.605	.513	.436	.371	.317	.270	.231	.198
18	.836	.700	.587	.494	.416	.350	.296	.250	.212	.180
19	.828	.686	.570	.475	.396	.331	.277	.232	.194	.164
20	.820	.673	.554	.456	.377	.312	.258	.215	.178	.149

Periods (n)	Interest rates (r)									
	11%	12%	13%	14%	15%	16%	17%	18%	19%	20%
1	.901	.893	.885	.877	.870	.862	.855	.847	.840	.833
2	.812	.797	.783	.769	.756	.743	.731	.718	.706	.694
3	.731	.712	.693	.675	.658	.641	.624	.609	.593	.579
4	.659	.636	.613	.592	.572	.552	.534	.516	.499	.482
5	.593	.567	.543	.519	.497	.476	.456	.437	.419	.402
6	.535	.507	.480	.456	.432	.410	.390	.370	.352	.335
7	.482	.452	.425	.400	.376	.354	.333	.314	.296	.279
8	.434	.404	.376	.351	.327	.305	.285	.266	.249	.233
9	.391	.361	.333	.308	.284	.263	.243	.225	.209	.194
10	.352	.322	.295	.270	.247	.227	.208	.191	.176	.162
11	.317	.287	.261	.237	.215	.195	.178	.162	.148	.135
12	.286	.257	.231	.208	.187	.168	.152	.137	.124	.112
13	.258	.229	.204	.182	.163	.145	.130	.116	.104	.093
14	.232	.205	.181	.160	.141	.125	.111	.099	.088	.078
15	.209	.183	.160	.140	.123	.108	.095	.084	.074	.065
16	.188	.163	.141	.123	.107	.093	.081	.071	.062	.054
17	.170	.146	.125	.108	.093	.080	.069	.060	.052	.045
18	.153	.130	.111	.095	.081	.069	.059	.051	.044	.038
19	.138	.116	.098	.083	.070	.060	.051	.043	.037	.031
20	.124	.104	.087	.073	.061	.051	.043	.037	.031	.026

astranti
financial training

Cumulative present value tables

This table shows the Present Value of £1 per annum, Receivable or Payable at the end of each year for n years:

$$\frac{1-(1+r)^{-n}}{r}$$

Periods (n)	Interest rates (r)									
	1%	2%	3%	4%	5%	6%	7%	8%	9%	10%
1	0.990	0.980	0.971	0.962	0.952	0.943	0.935	0.926	0.917	0.909
2	1.970	1.942	1.913	1.886	1.859	1.833	1.808	1.783	1.759	1.736
3	2.941	2.884	2.829	2.775	2.723	2.673	2.624	2.577	2.531	2.487
4	3.902	3.808	3.717	3.630	3.546	3.465	3.387	3.312	3.240	3.170
5	4.853	4.713	4.580	4.452	4.329	4.212	4.100	3.993	3.890	3.791
6	5.795	5.601	5.417	5.242	5.076	4.917	4.767	4.623	4.486	4.355
7	6.728	6.472	6.230	6.002	5.786	5.582	5.389	5.206	5.033	4.868
8	7.652	7.325	7.020	6.733	6.463	6.210	5.971	5.747	5.535	5.335
9	8.566	8.162	7.786	7.435	7.108	6.802	6.515	6.247	5.995	5.759
10	9.471	8.983	8.530	8.111	7.722	7.360	7.024	6.710	6.418	6.145
11	10.368	9.787	9.253	8.760	8.306	7.887	7.499	7.139	6.805	8.495
12	11.255	10.575	9.954	9.385	8.863	8.384	7.943	7.536	7.161	6.814
13	12.134	11.348	10.635	9.986	9.394	8.853	8.358	7.904	7.487	7.103
14	13.004	12.106	11.296	10.563	9.899	9.295	8.745	8.244	7.786	7.367
15	13.865	12.849	11.938	11.118	10.380	9.712	9.108	8.559	8.061	7.606
16	14.718	13.578	12.561	11.652	10.838	10.106	9.447	8.851	8.313	7.824
17	15.562	14.292	13.166	12.166	11.274	10.477	9.763	9.122	8.544	8.022
18	16.398	14.992	13.754	12.659	11.690	10.828	10.059	9.372	8.756	8.201
19	17.226	15.679	14.324	13.134	12.085	11.158	10.336	9.604	8.950	8.365
20	18.046	16.351	14.878	13.590	12.462	11.470	10.594	9.818	9.129	8.514

Periods (n)	Interest rates (r)									
	11%	12%	13%	14%	15%	16%	17%	18%	19%	20%
1	0.901	0.893	0.885	0.877	0.870	0.862	0685	0.847	0.840	0.833
2	1.713	1.690	1.668	1.647	1.626	1.605	1.585	1.566	1.547	1.528
3	2.444	2.402	2.361	2.322	2.283	2.246	2.210	2.174	2.140	2.106
4	3.102	3.037	2.974	2.914	2.855	2.798	2.743	2.690	2.639	2.589
5	3.696	3.605	3.517	3.433	3.352	3.274	3.199	3.127	3.058	2.991
6	4.231	4.111	3.998	3.889	3.784	3.685	3.589	3.498	3.410	3.326
7	4.712	4.564	4.423	4.288	4.160	4.039	3.922	3.812	3.706	3.605
8	5.146	4.968	4.799	4.639	4.487	4.344	4.207	4.078	3.954	3.837
9	5.537	5.328	5.132	4.946	4.772	4.607	4.451	4.303	4.163	4.031
10	5.889	5.650	5.426	5.216	5.019	4.833	4.659	4.494	4.339	4.192
11	6.207	5.938	5.687	5.453	5.234	5.029	4.836	4.656	4.486	4.327
12	6.492	6.194	5.918	5.660	5.421	5.197	4.968	4.793	4.611	4.439
13	6.750	6.424	6.122	5.842	5.583	5.342	5.118	4.910	4.715	4.533
14	6.982	6.628	6.302	6.002	5.724	5.468	5.229	5.008	4.802	4.611
15	7.191	6.811	6.462	6.142	5.847	5.575	5.324	5.092	4.876	4.675
16	7.379	6.974	6.604	6.265	5.954	5.668	5.405	5.162	4.938	4.730
17	7.549	7.120	6.729	6.373	6.047	5.749	5.475	5.222	4.990	4.775
18	7.702	7.250	6.840	6.467	6.128	5.818	5.534	5.273	5.033	4.812
19	7.839	7.366	6.938	6.550	6.198	5.877	5.584	5.316	5.070	4.843
20	7.963	7.469	7.025	6.623	6.259	5.929	5.628	5.353	5.101	4.870

astranti
financial training

CIMA BA3 Study Text

Chapter 18

Syllabus Referencing

Syllabus reference

A. Accounting Principles, Concepts and Regulations (10%)

Learning outcomes On completion of their studies, students should be able to:		Indicative syllabus content	Our ref.
Lead	**Component**		**Chapter and section**
1. explain the principles and concepts of financial accounting.	(a) explain the need for accounting records	I. Accounting records to be kept and their uses; concept of stewardship.	*Ch 1 s1*
	(b) identify the needs of different user groups	I. Uses of accounts and their information needs.	*Ch 1 s4*
	(c) distinguish between the purposes of financial and management accounts	I. Functions of financial and management accounts; purpose of accounting statements.	*Ch 1 s1*
	(d) explain capital and revenue, cash and profit, income and expenditure, assets and liabilities	I. Capital and revenue; cash and profit; income, expenditure, assets and liabilities.	*Ch 1 s5*
	(e) explain the underlying assumptions, policies and accounting estimates	I. Underlying assumptions, policies, accounting estimates; historical cost convention; qualitative characteristics of the Framework, elements of financial statements.	*Ch 6 s1* *Ch 6 s4* *Ch 1 s5*
	(f) identify the need for and information to be included in an integrated report	I. The principles and elements of the Framework for integrated reporting.	*Ch 15 s8*
	(g) describe the accounting equation	I. The accounting equation formula.	*Ch 2 s1*
	(h) explain the need for accounting codes	I. Use of coding in record keeping.	*Ch 3 s2*

2.	explain the impact of the regulatory framework on financial accounting.	(a)	explain the influence of legislation and accounting standards on published accounting information	I. Regulatory influence of company law; role of accounting standards; IASs and IFRSs; formats for published accounts.	*Ch 6 s2-3*

B. Recording Accounting Transactions (50%)

Learning outcomes On completion of their studies, students should be able to:			Indicative syllabus content	Our ref.
Lead		**Component**		**Chapter and section**
1. prepare accounting records.	(a)	prepare the books of prime entry	I. Record sales, purchase, income and expense transactions in the sales day book, purchase day book, cash book, returns books, and sales/purchase ledger.	Ch 3 s1-4
	(b)	apply the principles of double-entry bookkeeping	I. The accounting equation; double-entry bookkeeping rules; journal entries.	Ch 2 s1, s3 Ch 3 s2
	(c)	prepare nominal ledger accounts	I. Record all types of business transactions in nominal ledger accounts.	Ch 3 s5
	(d)	prepare the trial balance	I. Completing the trial balance from given ledger account balances.	Ch 4 s1-5
	(e)	explain the nature of accounting errors	I. Errors including those of principle, omission, and commission.	Ch 11 s1-3
	(f)	prepare accounting entries for the correction of errors	I. Journal entries and suspense accounts.	Ch 11 s4
	(g)	prepare accounting entries for non-current assets	I. In accordance with IAS 16 - acquisition, depreciation (straight line, reducing balance), revaluation, impairment and disposal of tangibles. II. In accordance with IAS 38 - intangibles and amortisation.	Ch 9 s1-8 Ch 10 s1-4
	(h)	prepare a non-current asset register	I. Information to be recorded in a non-current asset register.	Ch 9 s9
2. prepare accounting reconciliations.	(a)	prepare bank reconciliation statements	I. Reconciliation of the cashbook to the bank statement.	Ch 11 s5
	(b)	prepare petty cash statements under an imprest system	I. Using the imprest system for petty cash.	Ch 11 s5
	(c)	prepare sales and purchase ledger control account reconciliations	I. Reconciliation of sales and purchase ledger control accounts to sales and purchase ledgers.	Ch 11 s5

3.	prepare accounting entries for specific transactions.	(a)	calculate sales tax	I. Calculation of sales tax on all business transactions.	*Ch 5 s5*
		(b)	prepare accounting entries for sales tax	I. Accounting entries for sales tax. Note: no knowledge of any specific tax systems/ rules/rates will be required.	*Ch 5 s5*
		(c)	prepare accounting entries for payroll	I. Accounting entries for basic payroll information. Note: no knowledge of any specific income tax rules will be required.	*Ch 7 s2*
		(d)	prepare accounting entries for the issue of shares	I. Issue at full market price, rights issue and bonus issue.	*Ch 16 s4*

astranti
financial training

C. Preparation of Accounts for Single Entities (30%)

Learning outcomes On completion of their studies, students should be able to:			Indicative syllabus content	Our ref.
Lead	Component			Chapter and section
1. prepare accounting adjustments.	(a)	prepare accounting entries for accruals and prepayments	I. Calculations and journals for accruals and prepayments (income and expenses).	Ch 7 s1
	(b)	prepare accounting entries for irrecoverable debts and allowances for receivables	I. Prepare journals for irrecoverable debts and allowances for receivables from given information.	Ch 7 s3
	(c)	prepare accounting entries for inventories	I. In accordance with IAS 2 - calculation of the figure for closing inventory for inclusion in the financial statements (FIFO, LIFO and average cost) and the journal entry to record it.	Ch 8 s1-3
2. prepare manufacturing accounts.	(a)	prepare basic manufacturing accounts	I. Manufacturing accounts produced from given information. Note: No calculation of overheads and inventory balances is required.	Ch 12 s1-4
3. prepare financial statements for a single entity.	(a)	prepare financial statements from a trial balance	I. In accordance with IAS 1 - Statement of profit or loss and other comprehensive income; statement of financial position; statement of changes in equity.	Ch 4 s6-7
	(b)	prepare financial statements from incomplete records	I. Calculate missing numbers using the accounting equation, profit margins and mark-ups, receivables and payables ledgers, and cash and bank ledgers.	Ch 13 s1-3
	(c)	prepare a statement of cash flows	I. In accordance with IAS 7 - operating, investing and financing sections.	Ch 14 s1-6

D. Analysis of Financial Statements (10%)

Learning outcomes On completion of their studies, students should be able to:			Indicative syllabus content	Our ref.
Lead	**Component**			**Chapter and section**
1. identify information provided by accounting ratios.	(a)	identify the information provided by the calculation of accounting ratios	I. Information provided by accounting ratios.	*Ch 15 s1*
	(b)	identify reasons for the changes in accounting ratios	I. Reasons for the changes in accounting ratios.	*Ch 15 s1, 7*
2. calculate basic accounting ratios.	(a)	calculation of profitability ratios	I. Ratios: return on capital employed; gross, operating and net profit margins; non-current asset turnover.	*Ch 15 s3*
	(b)	calculation of liquidity ratios	I. Trade receivables collection period and trade payables payment period; current and quick ratios; inventory turnover.	*Ch 15 s4*
	(c)	calculation of risk ratios	I. Gearing and interest cover.	*Ch 15 s6-7*

Study Text reference

Astranti Study Text Chapter and Section		Syllabus referencing
Chapter	**Section**	**Based on the syllabus highlighted above.**
1. The Purpose of Financial Reporting	1. What is financial reporting? 2. What is a business? 3. Who does financial reporting? 4. Who uses financial statements? 5. Elements of the financial statements 6. The financial statements	A – 1(a) – I A – 1(a) – I A – 1(a) – I A – 1(b) – I A – 1(d) – I. A – 1(c) – I A – 1(c) - I
2. The Accounting System	1. The accounting equation 2. Ledger accounts 3. Double entry bookkeeping 4. Documentation and transactions 5. Benefits of accounting systems	A – 1(g) – I B – 1(b) – I B – 1(b) – I A – 1(a) – I A – 1(a) – I
3. The Bookkeeping Process	1. The bookkeeping process 2. Books of prime entry 3. Purchases and sales ledgers 4. Cash books 5. From daybooks to the nominal ledger 6. Reconciliation	B – 1(a) – I B – 1(a) – I B – 1(a) – I B – 1(a) – I; A – 1(h) - I B – 1(c) – I B – 2(a) – I; (b) -I; (c) - I
4. Producing a Trial Balance and Financial Statements	1. Balancing the books 2. Entering the transactions 3. Balancing asset accounts 4. Totalling the income and expense accounts Trial balance 5. The statement of profit or loss 6. Financial statements 7.	B – 1(d) – I B – 1(d) – I B – 1(d) – I B – 1(d) – I B – 1(d) – I C – 3(a) – I C – 3(a) – I
5. Recording Transactions	1. Introduction 2. Methods of transaction 3. Account types 4. Discounts 5. Sales tax 6. Corporation tax	B – 1(a) – I B – 1(a) – I B – 1(a) – I B – 1(a) – I B – 3(a) – I B – 3(b) – I
6. The Regulatory Framework	1. Assumptions of accounting 2. The regulatory framework 3. International Accounting Standards Board (IASB) 4. Qualitative characteristics of financial information 5. Governance and financial reporting	A – 2(a) – I A – 2(a) – I A – 2(a) – I A – 1(e) – I A – 1(a) - I
7. Accruals, Pay and Bad Debts	1. Accruals and prepayments 2. Employee pay 3. Bad debts and allowances	C – 1(a) – I B – 3(c) – I C – 1(b) – I

8.	Inventory	1.	Inventory	C – 1(c) – I
		2.	Measuring inventory	C – 1(c) – I
		3.	Components of cost	C – 1(c) - I
9.	Non-current Assets	1.	Assets	B – 1(g) – I
		2.	Capital and revenue	B – 1(g) – I
		3.	Recognition (initial measurement)	B – 1(g) – I
		4.	Subsequent measurement	B – 1(g) – I
		5.	Depreciation	B – 1(g) – I
		6.	Calculating depreciation	B – 1(g) – I
		7.	De-recognition	B – 1(g) – I
		8.	Comprehensive example	B – 1(g) – I
		9.	Non-current asset register	B – 1(h) - I
10.	Intangible Assets	1.	IAS 38 Intangible Assets	B – 1(g) – II
		2.	Recognition	B – 1(g) – II
		3.	Measurement	B – 1(g) – II
		4.	Accounting for amortisation	B – 1(g) - II
11.	Dealing with errors	1.	Errors	B – 1(e) – I
		2.	Preventing errors	B – 1(e) – I
		3.	Detecting errors	B – 1(e) – I
		4.	The correction of errors and suspense accounts	B – 1(f) – I
			Reconciliation statements	
		5.	Contra entries	B – 2(a) – I; (b) -I; (c) - I
		6.		B – 2(a) – I; (b) -I; (c) - I
12	The Manufacturing Account	1.	Introduction	C – 2(a) – I
		2.	Costs to include in the manufacturing account	C – 2(a) – I
			The layout of the manufacturing account	
		3.	The accounting system	C – 2(a) – I
		4.		C – 2(a) - I
13	Incomplete Records	1.	Missing figures	C – 3(b) – I
		2.	Cash and bank summaries	C – 3(b) – I
		3.	Gross profit mark-up and margin	C – 3(b) – I
14.	The Statement of Cash Flows	1.	The Statement of Cash Flows	C – 3(c) – I
		2.	Cash flow from operating activities	C – 3(c) – I
		3.	Cash flow from investing activities	C – 3(c) – I
		4.	Cash flow from financing activities	C – 3(c) – I
		5.	The Statement of Cash Flows: Full Statement	C – 3(c) – I
			Importance of the statement of cash flows	
		6.		C – 3(c) – I
15.	Interpreting Financial Statements	1.	Introduction	D – 1(a) – I
		2.	Example financial statements	D – 1(a) – I
		3.	Profitability ratios	D – 2(a) - I
		4.	Liquidity ratios	D – 2(b) - I
		5.	Efficiency ratios	D – 2(c) - I
		6.	Capital structure ratios	D – 2(c) - I
		7.	Ratio comparison	D – 1(a) - I
		8.	Integrated reporting	A – 1(f) - I

16.	Capital Structure	1.	Capital markets	$B - 3(d) - I$
		2.	Equity finance	$B - 3(d) - I$
		3.	Debt finance	$B - 3(d) - I$
		4.	Rights issues and Bonus issues	$B - 3(d) - I$
		5.	Dividends	$B - 3(d) - I$

Printed in Great Britain
by Amazon